SMARTER
NOT
HARDER

www.amplifypublishing.com

Smarter Not Harder: 17 Navy SEAL Maxims to Elevate Critical Thinking and Prosper in Business and Life

For more information, please contact:
Amplify Publishing
620 Herndon Parkway, Suite 320
Herndon, VA 20170
info@amplifypublishing.com

Library of Congress Control Number: 2021902390

CPSIA Code: PRV0421A

ISBN-13: 978-1-64543-167-1

Printed in the United States

To Jillian and Tristan

You are the master of your fate:
You are the captain of your soul.

Adapted from *Invictus* by William Ernest Henley

SMARTER

NOT

HARDER

17 NAVY SEAL MAXIMS TO ELEVATE
CRITICAL THINKING AND PROSPER
IN BUSINESS AND LIFE

DAVID SEARS

COMMANDER, US NAVY (SEAL), RET.

On July 23, 2020, I submitted my manuscript for review to the Department of Defense. On November 20, 2020, just shy of four months later, I received a letter stating that my manuscript was "cleared as amended." All amendments and black box redactions are at the specific direction of the Department of Defense, Defense Office of Prepublication and Security Review. In addition, the Department of Defense "requested" that I include the following statement: *The views expressed in this publication are those of the author and do not necessarily reflect the official policy or position of the Department of Defense or the US government.*

No kidding.

CONTENTS

AUTHOR'S NOTE 1

1   SMARTER, NOT HARDER 3

2   TIMING IS EVERYTHING 13

3   SHOOT, MOVE, AND COMMUNICATE 29

4   SPEED, SURPRISE, AND VIOLENCE OF ACTION......... 45

5   GET OFF THE X 61

6   TWO IS ONE, ONE IS NONE 73

7   CRAWL, WALK, RUN 89

8   THE MORE YOU SWEAT IN TRAINING,
THE LESS YOU BLEED IN WAR 107

9   IT PAYS TO BE A WINNER 123

10   WORK HARD, PLAY HARD 135

11   PAIN IS WEAKNESS LEAVING THE BODY 145

12   MIND OVER MATTER
(IF YOU DON'T MIND, IT DOESN'T MATTER) 157

13   NOTHING LASTS FOREVER.....................................171

14   NEVER QUIT 183

15   SLOW IS SMOOTH, SMOOTH IS FAST 195

16   IF YOU'RE NOT CHEATING, YOU'RE NOT TRYING....207

17   THE ONLY EASY DAY WAS YESTERDAY 223

ACKNOWLEDGMENTS...235

AUTHOR'S NOTE

Welcome to what I hope is the beginning of a better way of thinking. This book is intended to help you continue down the path of what should be a lifelong journey of continuing education and intellectual curiosity.

It doesn't need to be read from front to back. It can be taken as a series of small essays, with each chapter able to stand on its own. As a whole, the book is more than just the sum of its parts, but either approach to consuming these lessons works. Life doesn't happen in a straight line, and neither does this book. The chapters are loosely organized based on some prevalent themes. Chapters 2–5 discuss taking action; chapters 6–10 speak to teamwork and training; chapters 11–14 cover mental attitude; and chapters 15–17 address overarching approaches to thinking. There is overlap between chapters, and reflections of similar themes can be found in different maxims, just hit from a different angle. Read it cover to cover or jump around; it's up to you.

What this book *isn't* is a biography of my time in the SEAL Teams or a story about me. Rather, I use the maxims and stories from my experiences in the SEAL Teams as a jumping-off point to begin the conversation and stir your curiosity.

And that's what this book is meant to do: spur your interest and provide useful tips and ideas to get you started on your journey while also entertaining you a bit.

This book only scratches the surface. It is just the beginning. I'm not promising an overnight fix, a magic pill, or an algorithm or formula for success. Anyone who promises that is selling you snake oil. What I am promising is that this book will make you reflect on your own thinking, because how and what we think is how we learn. You still must do the hard work, but moving forward, you will be able to do it smarter.

Fair winds.

1

SMARTER, NOT HARDER

You've heard the saying "Work smarter, not harder." It's not exclusive to the SEAL Teams. In fact, it's a common phrase with a fairly obvious and straightforward message.

But like all the maxims in this book, we're going to look at its deeper meaning. In fact, the entire goal of our exploration will be to escape the obvious. To examine the true lessons behind the most popular sayings we regularly used during my twenty years in the United States Navy SEAL Teams and how I applied them when leading elite warriors into combat.

You can still hear these sayings today on the sands of Coronado, where every SEAL's training begins—at Basic Underwater Demolition SEAL training (BUD/S), one of the most difficult schools in all the military—and in war zones around the world wherever SEALs are deployed. We'll explore these sayings holistically, examining their meanings as part of a larger and more complex system rather than as independent and single-faceted clichés.

Doing so will be an exercise in thinking differently and more deeply. Going beneath the surface. Common thought processes and standard methods for solving problems will not be sufficient. We're going to practice looking at the world through different lenses and filters to achieve new insights, perspectives, and perceptions.

Many of the lessons within are counterintuitive. In some cases, the methodology of deliberation discussed is the opposite of what we've been taught our whole lives. Checking cognitive biases at the door will be required.

This starts with learning how to think smarter, not harder. Hence the title and first chapter. We're going to practice reading smarter, working smarter, living smarter, and playing smarter. These lessons can be applied to any arena. Part of thinking differently and more deeply means not limiting yourself to the status quo. It's about getting outside the norms and truly considering why you do what you do. And then doing it better.

Surface-level thinking is easy. Staying in your comfort zone is, well, comfortable. But it will get you nowhere. Obvious decision-making strategies won't separate you from the pack. You have to be able to adapt your way of thinking. Taking the path of least resistance merely gets you where everyone else has gone. That's never been my goal.

You learn pretty quickly in the SEAL Teams that to do something special, there are no shortcuts. The most rewarding path is usually the most difficult, and there are no shortage of clichés to remind you of that. We'll skip those. I'm not going out on a limb by saying easy isn't always better. My job is to show you how my career following and leading some of the most incredible humans on the planet in and out of combat taught me to skirt the obvious, straightforward way of looking at a problem in order to achieve maximum results. Doing so isn't easy or obvious, and there isn't a linear model that says if you do A, B, and C, you'll reach D. It takes practice, hard work, and an ability to get out of your comfort zone. Overcoming an obstacle isn't always about grit or sheer willpower; often it's about acting and thinking smarter.

Yes, every one of the maxims within, beginning with "Smarter, not harder," is a saying we used when I was a SEAL. But even within the walls of Naval Special Warfare Command, these maxims were and still are considered and practiced differently. This book expresses my views on them, how *I* see the world. Other SEALs and people may see and apply them differently, and that's OK.

But these sayings contributed to how I think to this day. They served as reminders to reflect on my own beliefs. Taken from small snippets of my experiences, meant to stir intellectual curiosity and get people to reflect on their own thinking. That starts with doing everything smarter instead of harder.

The explanation of this maxim begins like most of the maxims in this book: with a caveat and then a personal story. It is important not to take any of these phrases simply at face value or too literally. In each we will explore a deeper meaning. They are concise phrases that encompass a larger significance and need to be treated as such.

The way I see the larger meaning for this maxim is that hard work is assumed. It isn't really "Smarter *not* harder." It's "Smarter *along with* harder." *Nothing* can be accomplished without sacrifice and hard work. This maxim doesn't suggest hard work isn't required; it simply means it is not sufficient.

When I first made it to the Teams—this was pre–9/11—we still had a permanent presence in Panama, with some incredible training areas to hone our jungle warfare skill set. One of those areas was just north and west of the final canal locks that empty into the Pacific Ocean. Camp McFaul was an austere training area where we conducted everything from full mission profile live fire drills to jungle survival and land navigation exercises.

During one jungle warfare training block when I was a young ensign (junior officer), we were dropped off by a vehicle just north of Rodman Naval Base in two groups of eight men. Each squad was tasked with separately conducting a land navigation and patrolling exercise through the jungle to Camp McFaul. Total distance between start and finish: fifteen kilometers north as the crow flies, through some of the most gnarly terrain on the planet. If you made it five kilometers a day, it would be considered good time.

Patrolling in the jungle is an immense challenge. The going is slow, even during daytime. Ground foliage can vary depending on whether you're in an area of single, double, or triple canopy overhead. Finding a path often involves either cutting your way through with a machete or navigating in meandering curves to avoid the underbrush or ravines. Most cliffs aren't marked on maps, and they appear out of nowhere. The terrain is rife with black palm trees, which appear pretty and tropical like most palm trees do. But in the Panamanian jungles, the palm trees' trunks are covered with needles that can grow more than six inches long and are covered in bacteria. These painful suckers easily penetrate clothing, gloves, boots, and most definitely skin, causing injury and infection.

You usually can't see more than five or ten feet in front of you, even in the daytime. Then there are the creatures. Giant banana spiders as big as your face. Poisonous frogs and centipedes. Huge bushmasters, venomous snakes with a strike so powerful it's rumored they can break a femur. Fer-de-lances, vipers whose venom will easily kill a grown man. And the constant, unnerving cry of the howler monkey colonies making it sound like King Kong is chasing you through the jungle.

This was where we would be living and working for the next three weeks. The jungle is one of the most beautiful environments on the planet, but as outlined above can be extremely dangerous and unforgiving. Being tough and working hard would be necessary—but not enough—to make it through. We would need to be smart as well.

If you stumbled, you had to know not to reach out to catch yourself and run the risk of grabbing a black palm. We didn't sleep on the ground, instead getting in the trees or hanging a hammock when we rested. Sleeping off the ground was a necessity to keep fire ants, snakes, vampire bats, and other critters from taking a piece of you home with them. Since it only took hours for infection to take hold in the humid, bacteria-filled jungle, we needed to take care of cuts and scratches right away. With the heat and humidity, the rule of thumb was to hydrate and then hydrate some more.

Picking a route would be the most important and thoughtful piece. Decisions would have to be made. Did we take the shortest path, a straight line? Or did we try to navigate through the terrain and take the easier path, even if it was longer? What about schedule? Did we rest and only hike during certain times, or should we try to keep moving at all costs?

Those were just some of the things to consider when we set off on our three-to-four-day patrol to Camp McFaul. I led one squad; another officer was leading the other. To say that we had different mentalities and styles would be an extreme understatement.

My counterpart was definitely a hard man. He chose the head-on approach. He seemed to have a belief that the more difficult the path, the greater the reward. He chose to take his men on nearly a straight compass bearing and even tried patrolling at night. He was determined to bend the jungle to his will.

I had a different mentality, largely informed by taking advice from the guys around me who had experience there. I decided to listen to the jungle (and the guys who had "been there and done that") and let it tell me when and where to go. We would navigate in a general direction, patrolling around hills and avoiding ravines. We'd hunker down at night, then move out in the cooler dawn and dusk hours, slowing it down and resting during the peak heat.

This meant a meandering path and added a lot of extra kilometers to our patrol. We arrived at the camp just before dusk on the third day. Overall, our squad was in pretty good shape. We all appeared pretty fresh, and we hadn't had any major incidents. Our spirits were good.

The other squad hadn't arrived yet. So we cleaned up, set up camp, caught some delicious peacock bass for dinner, and settled in for a great night's sleep.

Late the next day, the other squad came stumbling into the camp. The looked like they had just completed a second Hell

Week. Guys were cut up, bug bitten from head to toe, limping, muttering, and cursing. After we let them cool down a bit, the stories started to come out. They had gone up and over every hill in front of them and down into each ravine. They even had to rig ropes at one point to get over a particularly nasty hill, an endeavor that took nearly all day. They tried to patrol at night until a couple guys fell into a thirty-foot ravine. They were lucky to be alive.

Their leader had been more concerned with doing things the intuitive way: straight ahead, the shortest route between points. But the hard way. Born out of either some misguided idea that harder was better, or just the simplicity of going straight. As a result, one squad ended up ready to train for the next three weeks, and one squad was left physically and mentally done before training even began.

The jungle, like life, requires that you work hard. There is no way around hard work. But it isn't sufficient to thrive. Both squads patrolled hard. But only one patrolled smart. It takes both to truly excel.

During my career, I saw guys work incredibly hard and not gain much traction. It brings to mind the saying "Practice makes perfect." We've all heard it. It implies that the more you practice or the harder you work at something, the better you will become at it. It's not true.

Deliberate, thoughtful, smart practice with feedback is what makes you better. With hard work, you may stumble on gains or progress, but if you combine it with smart work, your gains and successes will be accelerated.

If my goal was to run a marathon and I just went out and ran every day, I might eventually be able to complete twenty-six miles, but there would be a lot of wasted energy and more than likely injuries. But if I followed a designed running program, smartly ratcheted up mileage, incorporated speed work, kept track of heart rate variability and VO2 max, attended a clinic, and got a running coach, I would drastically exceed anything I could have achieved by only working hard.

I'll tell the story of another time we (thankfully) did things smarter rather than harder. Thinking differently and outside of the status quo saved us a lot of headache and probably some lives. It was right after Operation Iraqi Freedom had started in 2003. I was with Naval Special Warfare Development Group (DEVGRU), ███████████████████████████, at the time. We were part of the initial invasion of Iraq and found ourselves getting established at Baghdad International Airport.

As we began establishing an FOB (forward operating base) in downtown Baghdad to launch operations from and be closer to conventional forces, I made friends with some guys from various tank platoons and mechanized infantry battalions in the army's Third Infantry Division.

The guys from Third Division had seen some fierce combat against Saddam's military forces and had been taking serious casualties from rocket-propelled grenade (RPG) attacks. By hanging their rucksacks outside their Bradley Fighting Vehicles as they marched north up the Tigris–Euphrates river valley, these guys had unwittingly stumbled on some outside-the-box protection for the Bradleys. They found that instead of impacting directly into the vehicle, the RPGs would detonate when hitting the rucksack and not penetrate their armor. Talk about thinking smarter—the few inches between their vehicle and detonation meant that the molten jet formed from the shape charge in the RPG was dissipated sufficiently to not be able to penetrate the relatively thin armored skin of the Bradley. However, the downside was they were losing all their clothes and socks. Wearing the same pair of socks for weeks on end in the desert sand and heat is utterly miserable. In fact, that's how we became friends with some of these guys: we rounded up and gave them extra socks.

This was in the beginning of the war, before the insurgency, and there were still pockets of Saddam's infamous fedayeen fighters and plenty of the Republican Guard still fighting. We'd gotten intelligence there was a fedayeen stronghold on the outskirts of town. The hardcore of the hardcore, ready to fight to the death. Our higher command immediately went to work making plans to send my squadron to assault their compound.

My guys and I were dumbfounded. We were a precision tool, designed for raids on high-value targets and hostage rescues. Why would they send us to assault this place? It was like using a scalpel when a chainsaw was called for. I think headquarters was just looking for us to assault it because it was there. But I knew from my new friends in the armored division that there was a smarter way. We didn't have to make it hard.

These were fortified, vicious combatants ready to fight to the death. It seemed dumb to me to match up with them when we didn't have to. I mentioned my new friends to the head shed (leadership). I suggested, "Why don't we just roll up there with a bunch of tanks and invite the bad guys out to play? We don't even need to be there." We knew these guys were looking for a fight. We didn't need to give them a fair one.

So that's exactly what happened. We turned the mission over to the guys from Third Division with their armor and really big guns, and they crushed it. Later, they told me that when they showed up, the fedayeen came rushing out to fight their tanks and Bradleys with rifles and grenades. You can guess how that went for the bad guys.

As I already said, the idea behind this book is to get you to think differently and more deeply about everything you're doing in life. I want to encourage you to look at the world through a different lens. Embrace critical and creative thinking. At the core of "smarter, not harder" is the implication that thinking—your mind and mental abilities—is the true key to success, the ability to overcome, excel, and prosper in all aspects of life. Relationships, business, sports, academics, you name it. The physical part is the easy part. It's a given that hard work is an absolute prerequisite to success, but it's not sufficient. Lots of people work hard. What differentiates the successful is how smart they are at working hard.

2

TIMING IS EVERY-THING

I lowered my night vision goggles and looked out the window. Not twenty-five feet below, the Iraqi desert skimmed beneath the wheels of our MH-47 helicopter. Flashes of green light—antiaircraft and small-arms fire directed at our flying convoy—streaked across my view. I raised my night vision goggles and looked back inside the helicopter. A low red light allowed me to just barely make out twenty or so of my fellow SEAL operators in full MOPP gear—the protective suit you wear in toxic chemical, biological, radiological, or nuclear warfare environments—hurtling toward war.

President George W. Bush had launched Operation Iraqi Freedom just days earlier, and now the SEAL Team █ troop I commanded sat shoulder to shoulder flying to a suspected weapons of mass destruction (WMD) facility near the Iraq/Syria border.

We were tasked with confirming or denying the presence of WMDs, in this case in a suspected biological weapons manufacturing and/or storage site.

I scribbled on the illuminated lightboard (lum board) in my lap and held it up for my guys to see. "Twenty minutes out." I received a round of thumbs-ups in return, but it remained fairly quiet on board aside from the constant drone of the engine and some occasional small talk. It was our way of breaking either the tension or boredom, though it was usually hard to tell which. Everyone continued to prep gear and check maps, occasionally looking out the side windows or nodding off for short bits of sleep. I stayed focused on the headquarters communications channel, where I was getting regular intel updates on the target from the joint operations center, hundreds of miles away in the comfort of their air-conditioned tents. At the same time, I was in constant communication with the pilots of our bird, who were updating me on time to target and any intelligence coming from the other helos in our formation.

As we made our final approach, I learned two other MH-47s, the large transport choppers we and our two sister troops were traveling in, along with MH-60 Blackhawks carrying a Ranger element, were taking heavy fire on insert. That's what we would be flying into.

"Three minutes out, target is hot" I wrote on the lum board. Check.

As soon as I lowered the board, a strange, dull pinging sound could be heard over the engines. We looked around, wondering what the sound was. Someone called out loud enough to be heard over the engines, "Dude, those are rounds hitting the helo." There was no panic or surprise in his voice; he was just stating a fact. The pings grew in frequency, and we began to notice some new air-conditioning in the aircraft's skin. The enemy rounds were coming through.

Ping, ping, ping. Nothing we could do but make ourselves smaller and hope one of those rounds didn't have our name on it. That's why we hated helicopters; we had no control.

Next to me, my buddy continued his prep. He bent down to relace his boot or something—I'm not even sure what he was doing—but it caused him to lean all the way forward. A dull *ping ping* in rapid succession caused me to look in his direction. When he sat back up, I chuckled and pointed to the wall behind him.

He turned and saw two new bullet holes right where his head had been. If he hadn't leaned over at that exact moment, it would have been a really bad situation. He raised his eyebrows and shrugged as if to say, "What are you gonna do?"

And he was right. In that instance, it was blind luck that he hadn't been hit. Life is full of happenstances like that. A round through a helo was pretty common in my world. And there are just as many stories of RPGs going straight through a helicopter's skin and going out the other side without exploding.

Sometimes, timing is just blind luck. Always, luck is what you make of it. It's been said that luck is the intersection of opportunity and preparation. But it's more than that. It's not just *what* you do with an opportunity: it's also about recognizing *when* to act on it. That's why timing is everything.

When tackling a problem, the first things people invariably consider are the "what" and "how." "Why" and "where" usually follow. But for some reason, "when" doesn't rank high on the list of considerations—but it should. In matters of confronting change or being presented with opportunities, asking the "when" question is just as important as figuring out the who, what, why, and how.

Without understanding that concept, even subconsciously, I might never have had a career in the SEAL Teams.

I went to Boston University on a navy ROTC scholarship. My plan was always to become a naval officer. What was unclear was in what capacity. I had dreamed of being a pilot as a kid, but sub–twenty-twenty vision eliminated that option. I wasn't really interested in being stuck on a ship. I had heard of the Navy SEALs, but I assumed the same vision issue precluded me from that field. So I coasted through college and ROTC, not the best student, not the best midshipman, unsure of what exactly I would do in the navy after I graduated. Until one night in my junior year when my roommate's stepbrother met us for drinks at the BU Pub, a local watering hole in Boston.

His name was also Dave, and he was attending Harvard Medical School just down the road from BU. He had just gotten out of the navy, where he had been—you guessed it—a SEAL.

As we sat down with a round of beers, Dave asked me what I planned to do in the navy after graduating college. I answered honestly, explaining that I wasn't sure. I was already a civilian scuba diver, so I said maybe I'd be a navy diver or EOD (explosive ordinance disposal) technician. I knew I didn't want to do a normal desk job or be stationed in the fleet. He agreed wholeheartedly, saying that he could never have gone those routes either.

"The rest of the navy sucks for people like us," he told me. "Everything except for the SEAL Teams. Why the hell wouldn't you go SEAL Teams?"

"I'd love to," I answered. "But I don't have twenty-twenty vision."

He looked at me like I was crazy. "You don't need twenty-twenty to join the Teams. You need like twenty-forty or twenty-seventy."

I was shocked. I had just made an assumption that you needed perfect vision. There is an important lesson here about questioning your assumptions that we'll get into in later chapters. But the bottom line is that assumptions can turn into "facts" without you even realizing it.

The next day, I started researching the requirements to go to BUD/S, the legendary school where SEAL training begins. Of the well-screened candidates who are selected to attend BUD/S, only about 20 percent make it through. I discovered Dave was right about the vision requirement. I reached back out to him with questions about what it took to become a SEAL. He offered his help and advice. I took it. I started working out with him, focusing on the things that would help me make it through training, like swimming, running, and lifting with him in his gym at Harvard. I absorbed the little tips he'd offer but learned mostly by observing. I already had a strong swimming background, and he taught me the combat swimmer sidestroke, which you have to use in BUD/S. He would offer insights here and there while we ran the stairs at Harvard Stadium or had a beer at whatever dive bar I could convince him to meet me at. His advice was more centered on training than on how to get through BUD/S; that guidance was simple and didn't change: "Just don't quit." There was no silver bullet, and he wasn't offering one.

Over the next couple of years, with Dave's support, I worked my ass off so when I was given the opportunity to attend BUD/S, I wouldn't fail. And I didn't.

I can't say for certain that if I had never met Dave, I wouldn't have had a successful career in the Teams. But I absolutely had to take advantage of the serendipitous timing of when I met him. I didn't only focus on "how" to prepare for BUD/S. I had to look at "when." And not just deciding when to apply or attend. The "when" had to be accounted for in my entire strategy.

I had to wait to reach back out to Dave only after I had done my research; I couldn't just instantly ask a bunch of dumb questions and expect him to give me the answers. I had to select strategic times to ask for help; he was a Harvard med student and incredibly busy. Had I bombarded him with questions and daily requests to work out, he probably wouldn't have helped me. I had to fit into *his* schedule. Take advantage when he was going for a run, be flexible around his lifting schedule, know when he had exams. When did he go out? When did he study? When was he headed home for the holidays? I had to consider all these things. Then I had to put in the work and incorporate those different aspects of timing into a strategy to take advantage of meeting Dave.

Those stories are two basic and straightforward examples of utilizing and optimizing timing. But there are more advanced scales, scopes, and perspectives to consider. It's imperative to have those aligned, zooming in and out on both the short and long term when considering timing.

The two most important "whens" to consider are the *tactical* when and the *strategic* when. Any good plan is going to take both into account while simultaneously understanding the effect that they have on each other. Your end goal will determine which "when" should dominate your planning and decision-making. But first you must understand the difference between the two.

The simplest way of differentiation is to think of the *tactical* when as more immediate and short term. A day trader interested in quick gains is more focused on the tactical than on a long-term strategy with many moving parts. He's not concerned about the impact the sale of a stock will have on his retirement account, or if holding a position longer will limit his end-of-year tax exposure. He's in it for a quick hit, then moves on to an unrelated trade. Warren Buffett and your retirement advisor take longer views. Their decision-making process for buying and selling equities still has to be made every day (tactical) but incorporated into the overall goal of a well-rounded, reliable portfolio that takes the long view. That's the *strategic* when.

The strategic when is more long term than the tactical and often can be counterintuitive. Take a company releasing a new product. It makes perfect sense for there to be a tendency to rush good ideas to market, to get ahead of the competition and capture new market share. It's one of the core ideas behind the "minimum viable product" philosophy often found in the software industry. Get the product in front of early adopters with minimum expense to get feedback and then make adjustments.

In software, this might make sense. However, failing to take both the long term and the short term into account could lead to costly missteps. A consumer products company may equate this to designing and launching individual successful products only to later have them removed from their product line. They become out of sync or no longer fit with the product mix. Considering how you want your product mix, margins, and brand positioning to look five years from now versus next quarter will lead to avoiding costly R and D and tooling investments that ultimately turn out to be counterproductive.

Public companies especially can be beholden to tactical timing rather than strategic. They regularly prioritize short-term profits around executive bonuses and reporting to Wall Street, hurting the overall health and mission of the company. In fact, the chairman of Berkshire Hathaway, Warren Buffett, and the CEO of JPMorgan Chase, Jamie Dimon, have both gone on record advocating for public companies to stop quarterly estimates and reports. A *Wall Street Journal* opinion piece quoted them as saying, "Quarterly earning guidance often leads to an unhealthy focus on short-term profits at the expense of long-term strategy, growth, and sustainability." This means at best companies may shift focus away from investing in their people, research and development, or technology; at worst they could be motivated to fudge numbers or engage in unethical business practices to deliver the short-term earnings they forecast.

I saw our commanders and the leadership in Afghanistan fall victim to the tactical-versus-strategic issue all the time. Even good leaders could fail to recognize their own bias and fall victim to ignoring the strategic or long-term timing of decisions and actions—namely, ignoring other factors' timing and only focusing on their own.

US combat deployments have a time limit on them. Operators can be in country for anywhere from six months to a year. In some cases, senior leaders can deploy for up to two years, but everyone's deployment has a shelf life. And to their credit, most people want to make as big of an impact and get as much done as possible while over there. That sense of urgency, however, could mean that in the rush to take the fight to the enemy, strategic timing was discounted or outright ignored when planning missions or implementing policies.

Again, the "how" and "where" were always covered: a squadron, battalion, or platoon would insert via helicopter, land-based vehicle, or foot patrol. They would use intelligence to find the target, figure out the insert and extract locations, and set the stage for the operation. Even the tactical timing was considered. (I won't go into too many tactical details, in the interest of safety and security, but it's common knowledge that we tried to hit targets at night when the enemy was asleep, and darkness allowed us to utilize our technology and weaponry advantages.) There were all sorts of tactical whens to consider: day versus night, mealtime, prayer time, holiday or not holiday, phase of the moon (sometimes a full moon is advantageous; sometimes a new moon is better). The bottom line is that if we could (sometimes time-sensitive targets or targets that moved frequently required different time calculations), we took advantage of the tactical when as best we could. But the strategic timing was all too often missed. Planners would only take their own timing into account, forgetting the timing of other necessary actors.

It's no secret that most of the world's poppies, the main ingredient in heroin, are grown and harvested in Afghanistan and are a large source of funding for the Taliban. But another, unintended effect of the poppy harvest greatly impacted our operations: late every spring, a certain portion of the Afghan army, whom we'd spent so much time and money training, would suddenly disappear to go home and help their families harvest the plant. Boom, just like that, they'd be gone, no warning or timetable for their return. "I'll be back, inshallah" was as good as we could hope for. These unannounced exits would leave their US partners, who relied heavily on their tribal knowledge during operations, high and dry.

I remember being given a reconnaissance mission from higher-ups one deployment. My team was living in a decent-sized safe house compound in the middle of Jalalabad, and we were tasked with driving toward the Khyber Pass on the Afghan/Pakistan border and then heading south across the plains and into the mountains to check some of the remote villages for Taliban and al-Qaeda fighters. We had a strong contingent of Afghan army quasi–special operations guys that we had trained extensively and conducted operations with whom we actually trusted. On this mission we would depend on them to take the pulse of these villages and interview the village elders, getting an idea of where the bad guys were and what was going on in the area. Intel that we couldn't easily get without them.

That morning, my alarm went off well before daybreak. I made coffee and started to police my personal gear before rechecking the team gear that had been prepped the night before. Five Toyota Hiluxes, two with heavy machine guns in the bed, had been rigged with ballistic blankets over the doors and on the floorboards. We had RPGs and a couple of LAW rockets (Light Anti-tank Weapon) loaded up, extra ammo, some food, and plenty of water. Going out would be me, two other SEALs, an OGA (other government agency) guy, and about twenty of our Afghan soldiers. I met with my chief and went over the plan one more time, discussing any last-minute changes and reviewing contingency plans.

"Dave," he told me, "a bunch of these guys aren't here."

"What do you mean 'aren't here'?" I said. "Where are they?"

"Not sure. I'll check with the terp."

When the chief came back, he informed me that at least five of our Afghan soldiers had gone home to help their families harvest poppy crops. They'd be back in a month. "Inshallah."

These were guys whom we had trained and operated with.

Guys we trusted, which was an incredibly valuable commodity when dealing with Afghan nationals. Now we'd have to replace them with guys we didn't know. That was enough to make the hair stand up on the back of your neck.

Green-on-blue attacks, or attacks on US forces by the supposed friendly Afghan soldiers we were working with, were a real concern. Operating with Afghans we didn't know and trust meant we had a whole new set of issues to consider outside of the mission. I knew we'd all be on edge, watching them closely. When patrolling, we'd have to take into consideration where they were at all times. Sometimes we'd keep them up front, and other times we'd have them take up the rear, depending on terrain and situation. But there really is no optimal place to put someone you aren't sure you can trust. This meant moving slower. Rather than being singularly focused on getting the job done, a portion of our attention would be on the replacement Afghan soldiers and where they were. The Afghans' sudden departure was going to seriously impact our ability to complete the mission safely, all because our higher-ups hadn't taken our Afghan partners' timing into account.

My chief and I discussed whether we should still conduct the operation. But the mission had already been green-lit, and we weren't in the business of passing up approved missions. Something about making the most of the time you had in country. We quickly decided that we could still accomplish the mission, but we'd have to limit its scope. By taking untrained Afghan soldiers we didn't know, there was no way we could stay out overnight. Aside from the trust factor, they had no night vision capabilities and didn't know our tactics and procedures. For example, we had trained our Afghan soldiers that if we got ambushed in the vehicles, we would patrol through the contact and take the fight to the enemy at a location of our choosing. These untrained guys would stop the vehicles at the first sign of contact, get out, and head for the high ground to fight. That sounds intuitive, but as we'll learn in a later chapter, it's important to "get off the X." If we got ambushed with these new guys, there was a real risk they'd stop a vehicle and block the road for the rest of the convoy, putting us all in a bad fighting position. I wasn't willing to risk my men needlessly, but the job still needed to get done.

So we rolled out just before daybreak in the Hiluxes with Afghans we didn't know, headed for remote mountains about fifty miles southeast of our safe house in Jalalabad. Normally I'd have had the Afghans drive, but that day I put my SEALs behind the wheel to ensure there were no mistakes. The road leaving Jbad was a smooth, paved highway, but about halfway to our destination, we turned off onto a dirt road, the farmland flat and green all around. As the elevation rose, the terrain quickly changed. The road became rocky. We drove through streambeds and rutted dirt roads. Soon we were in the mountains, going up and down valleys. Every so often a jinga truck, these huge dump trucks decorated to the nines with colorful paint and baubles hanging everywhere, would pass us, hauling illegal firewood or other contraband from Pakistan into Afghanistan. This is when I relied on my trusted Afghan soldiers—they could tell by looking at a jinga driver if there was anything suspicious. If there was, we'd stop them and search their load, oftentimes finding weapons or explosives being hauled back and forth across the border.

But that day we only stopped a few, finding nothing. No intel at the villages we visited either. My chief and I decided we should get back to the safe house before dark, so we decided to make a tiny village poking off the edge of a mountaintop our last stop.

There was a different energy in the air as we pulled into the village. The people looked at us with suspicion. Women started ushering the children into the huts, a sure sign something was up. This was a spot where I'd usually rely on my trusted Afghans. The village elder came out, an old, gnarled man with leathery skin and a long white beard. He didn't look friendly and wouldn't say much to our terp (interpreter). He told us we were the first Americans to visit the village and wouldn't say much more. My men were spread out doing their jobs, but we were thin. If we'd had our normal contingent, we would have felt safer. Something out of the ordinary might have been noticed, or maybe someone else could have gotten the elder to give us more information.

The chief and I decided to be cautious and cut the visit short, without finding any weapons caches or bad guys. I don't know that our regular guys would have turned up any Taliban or al-Qaeda, but when every tiny detail could mean the difference between life and death, being without them certainly handicapped us. I'm fairly certain that the operation could have been more successful, and we could have gone deeper and stayed out longer, if we had patrolled that area just a couple of weeks after the harvest.

Today American manufacturing companies are getting burned for failing to take strategic timing into account. Between the tariff wars and COVID-19, any American company with a heavy presence in China is suffering. They fell victim to overemphasizing short-term profits instead of long-term sustainability.

Several years ago China opened their doors to American companies with great aplomb. Being a Communist country, China isn't beholden to labor laws or human rights rules. They happily leveled villages to build plants for American companies, providing cheap labor and swift infrastructure. Tactically, the arrangement worked perfectly for the American companies. They were making money hand over fist by moving their operations to China. But they didn't take some big long-term unknowns into account: What if the political climate changed? What if a tariff war between the two countries meant importing their products back to American customers became unprofitable? What if a global pandemic originated in China? They would be screwed, that's what. By only focusing on what was right in front of them—favorable business conditions and short-term profits—those companies missed the bigger picture. And they're paying for it now.

There is nothing wrong with planning tactically. The key is to be aware you are doing it, not mistake it for strategic planning, and know the difference. Ask yourself out loud if your strategy is centered around a long-term "when" or a short-term "when." Better yet, is it taking both into account?

Once I got to BUD/S, the importance of timing was quickly impressed upon me in almost everything we did. But one evolution that every SEAL candidate is intimately familiar with summed it up beautifully: surf passage.

In BUD/S, students were divided into boat crews based on height, six to eight men per crew. During surf passage, each boat crew had to paddle their boat out past the breakers, usually "dump boat" by getting out and flipping it upside down, then right it, get back in, paddle parallel to the shoreline for a while, then paddle back in. Sounds simple, right?

Not so much. Keep in mind, this was in the cold Pacific Ocean outside San Diego and often done at night. Waves can easily reach six feet or higher. If you didn't time your paddle out—or your paddle in—correctly, you would end up in a world of hurt. I saw plenty of broken bones and near drownings from boat crews getting crushed by waves because they didn't time it correctly.

The key was timing the waves and sets. You wanted to wait until there was a lull, then paddle through the white water as swiftly as possible before the next set came. But you couldn't wait too long—you were racing the other boat crews, and as we'll learn later, it pays to be a winner. Each boat crew had to weigh the tactical when—waiting for a break in the waves—with the strategic when—not risking losing the race by waiting too long. And they had to do it as a team. I can't think of a better—or simpler— example of taking all aspects of timing into account than surf passage.

As with most things in life, those who understood how to properly take advantage of timing excelled and won. Those who didn't never made it through BUD/S and onto the SEAL Teams.

3

SHOOT, MOVE, AND COMMUNICATE

It was late March 2003 in the never-ending desert along the Iraq/
Saudi Arabia border. As usual, I woke up on our FOB (forward
operating base) covered in a thin coating of powdery red desert
sand. The large tent I shared with my troop, set up with sleeping areas for the ten to fifteen of us along with space for our
kit (gear), did little to keep the fine sand out of everything, no
matter what we did to prevent it. I was downing a bottle of water
when one of my guys unzipped the opening and stepped inside,
saying with a pretty urgent tone in his voice, "Dave, Boss needs
to see you right now." I gave him a thumbs-up with one hand
while finishing the water with the other, then threw on a shirt
and headed to the squadron commander's tent.

Our entire head shed, or leadership team, was beginning to
gather when I arrived, making everyone wonder what was up.
We had been reviewing plans and rehearsing to hit a target deep

behind enemy lines over the past few days, and our best guess was that the complicated operation had changed or the timeline been bumped up.

We quickly learned that the rushed briefing was not at all what we were expecting. Our task force had just received credible intelligence that Jessica Lynch, an American soldier who had been taken prisoner of war by Saddam Hussein's fedayeen after her supply convoy was ambushed the week before, was being held captive at a hospital on the west side of Nasiriyah. Our squadron was tasked with rescuing her, and we had limited time to create a mission plan and conduct the rescue. We had no idea how long she would be there or what shape she was in. The operation would be incredibly complex and was getting more so by the minute. Hundreds of factors would have to be taken into account, including manpower, weapons, vehicles, routes, and timing, while SEALs, Army Rangers, Air Force CCT and PJs (Combat Controllers and Pararescue), helicopters, fixed-wing aircraft, and drones would all be taking part in the rescue. Communicating properly between so many different forces and entities would be its own challenge. These disparate parts immediately got to work, moving at full speed.

The quick organization of manpower and flurry of planning must have looked tumultuous from the outside, but with everyone taking care of their individual and team responsibilities, it was an organized chaos. We worked throughout the night, bringing all the pieces together cohesively to form a detailed mission plan whose sum was certainly greater than its parts.

Without sleep, our twenty-two-vehicle convoy left Tallil Air Base near Nasiriyah around eleven the next morning. I was the ground assault force commander for the operation, meaning I would be the one responsible for getting this mass of firepower and men where they were supposed to be when they were supposed to be there. I was in one of the up-armored Humvees, the second vehicle in the convoy. The Second Marine Expeditionary Brigade had offered us two Abrams tanks, and when someone offers you tanks, you generally take them. Also in the convoy were five more up-armored Hummers with heavy weapons, carrying SEALs from my squadron; four Pandurs (begrudgingly loaned to us by our army brethren), heavily armored wheeled personnel carriers with heavy machine gun turrets, driven and manned by SEALs from my squadron; plus eleven more Humvees of Rangers and a mortar truck to provide a blocking force. In all, there were about 120 men in our convoy, plus an additional troop of assaulters that would helicopter directly to the target, and additional Rangers that would land in helos about five hundred meters away to provide additional firepower after the initial assault. As I said, lots of moving parts.

We couldn't take a direct route to the hospital where we believed Lynch was being held because it was heavily defended by the Iraqi Army and fedayeen. The road was a natural choke-point, making it a veritable "death avenue." We'd have to make our way north up the eastern side of the city, then head back down through the west side of the city, doing our best to skirt enemy forces. It would be a long drive around Nasiriyah—about eight hours—but the route was supposed to be relatively secure until we neared the hospital. The marines had already subdued the majority of the city during the Battle of Nasiriyah the week prior, and all that was supposed to be left were sporadic pockets of fedayeen and Republican Guard holdouts.

Our convoy needed to reach the hospital within seconds of the helicopter assault force, which would land in Blackhawks at the front door of the hospital. Snipers would be inserted on the roof by Little Birds (MH-6 helicopters) to provide overwatch, while a QRF (quick reaction force) of Rangers would be in helos about a quarter mile away.

Per the mission plan, it was dark as we approached the hospital in the early hours of April Fool's Day. The trip had been mostly uneventful, but as we made the final turn west toward the hospital, with less than a half mile to go, small-arms fire broke out all around us. One of the first rounds smashed into my vehicle's windshield right at head level. Luckily the armored glass held.

The scene immediately became chaotic; it was our job to bring order to it. Our shooters returned fire while the tanks peeled off to provide external security and secure the outer perimeter of the hospital. My SEALs started laying down suppressive fire from the Humvee turrets and rocking off Mark 19 grenade launchers, twin 240 mounted machine guns, and .50 cals, sending rounds wherever they thought the shooting was coming from. We continued moving toward the target, where we needed to augment the assault team landing in the helos. The whole time, I continued communicating with all the different elements, moving them where they could be best utilized.

"*One*, this is *four*, I've got huge gates closed at the entrance! Whaddya wanna do?!" came a radio transmission from my lead vehicle.

We were cruising along at forty miles per hour, so I told him, "Ram it!" He smashed through the gates, and our entire contingent poured into the hospital compound. We positioned the vehicles to provide security along the east and south walls and moved personnel on foot to cover the rest of the perimeter security. We needed to make sure we could protect the landing helos, including one that would take the POW to freedom. Everyone piled out of the vehicles, maneuvering and returning fire wherever targets were found.

The night lit up with infrared laser sights and tracer fire through my night vision goggles, reminiscent of a surreal Pink Floyd concert. The Rangers shot up a storm, blowing transformers and pretty much bringing destruction to everything in their path. My swim buddy and I dismounted and lay on the ground next to our vehicle but couldn't find anything worth shooting at. Suddenly, he called out, "Hey, someone's shooting at us from behind! Get under the vehicle." When we tried to take cover underneath the Hummer, we couldn't fit. Between my body armor, radios, and the rest of my kit, there just wasn't enough room to squeeze under the cover of the armored vehicle. Rounds were impacting the curb near us and the road behind us. Time to move.

We maneuvered toward the rest of our team while I communicated with my chief. They had perimeter security established, so we made our way into the hospital, moving to advantageous positions while covering each other. I'm not sure how much enemy resistance there actually was, but whoever had been firing at us was quickly and massively overwhelmed, and most of the shooting soon stopped.

By the time we entered the hospital, the lead component of the assault team had already found Lynch, and the medics were stabilizing her and taking her out. I continued repositioning forces, but for the most part, order had been restored. Time to leave. Then I got word from our snipers on the roof that they had spotted what appeared to be some shallow graves outside the compound. We knew that there were other POWs and KIAs who had been taken when the supply convoy had been ambushed, and we thought the graves might belong to them.

We made the decision to stay on target with the ground assault force, while the helicopter assault force would return to Tallil airfield. These were our brothers-in-arms, and they needed to be repatriated to their families, alive or dead. We repositioned security around the gravesites, dug up the remains, and brought them back to base, where arrangements were made to repatriate them to their final resting spot in the United States. It wasn't part of the original mission, but we had to be flexible and overcome mitigating circumstances to truly achieve our objective, even if that objective was altered along the way.

The Jessica Lynch rescue is a classic example of utilizing the principles of shoot, move, and communicate. The entire mission—from planning, logistics, and execution, to altering the mission plan and getting everyone back to base safely—was a multifaceted orchestration requiring constant repositioning and dynamic interactions between all parties. Ultimately, we shot, moved, and communicated well enough to successfully complete the mission.

That's what this maxim teaches us: how to shoot, move, and communicate to bring order to chaotic events, allowing us to win the event. For the majority of people reading this, these lessons aren't going to be utilized in combat. In the civilian world, these steps translate to "acting" and "adjusting" while communicating with both ourselves (internally) and the people around us.

When you find yourself in an immediate-crisis-type situation, using this this maxim as a first principle can help get you back to a stable place. Act, adjust, and communicate. Then you can take time to develop a new route, path, or strategy. You'll apply this concept when, say, you're starting a new business or training for a triathlon. Your "shooting" will be strategically or tactically acting in response to external influences. "Moving" means adjusting to the information coming in, which will be chaotic or sudden. And then you must communicate, both to your team and to any outside stakeholders or influencers, like customers and employees. This means taking measures to ensure the who, what, when, why, and where are transmitted clearly and, more importantly, received in the same manner.

These steps should be taken when confronting any situation you consider chaotic or sudden, disorderly events like a car accident, natural disaster, or active shooter. Events can also be less tangible, like the death of a loved one, losing your job, or going through a divorce. In either case, the idea is to get yourself to a steady place where other tools can be brought to bear. But before doing so, you must move out of a hectic and chaotic space and into one of stability.

Your initial actions should be positive ones that put you on a vector toward stability and order. Then you can take the time to evaluate and think more deliberately through your next moves, adjusting accordingly in response to the feedback you receive from your initial actions. Overlaid on top of this is the ever-present need for communication. The communication has to happen in two forms: transmitting and receiving. You need to be open to receiving incoming information that helps you adjust, and you need to transmit your intentions and the vector that you're moving along to everyone in your team.

Like all our maxims, these steps aren't simply checked off a list and discarded. When you find yourself under "immediate enemy fire," take action, observe, and then sense the results to adjust your *next* action based upon your observations. You may be repeating several of these steps. Rinse and repeat until you find yourself in a more orderly system and out of immediate danger. Do the same for each subset in the event. Remember, every event has other, smaller events happening at the same time. And it's important to follow the maxim when dealing with each.

For example, on the Jessica Lynch mission, getting the initial intelligence was an external event that we had to immediately analyze and adjust to. That was the first "chaotic event." We had to quickly come up with a mission plan. We had to organize resources. We had to get those resources where they needed to go. We had to execute the plan, as well as consider the thousands of other data points that make every event fluid.

However, there is an initial, unspoken piece to this maxim (probably because "shoot, move, and communicate" sounds cooler and rolls off the tongue more smoothly) that we imme-diately executed on and should never be discounted: *thinking.* Before you act, adjust, and communicate, it's imperative you pause and take inventory of the situation. Only then can you respond properly. While it might sound obvious, if *thinking* before taking action is ignored, it can lead to disaster. Shoot-ing before considering your environment is never a good thing. This thought process could take a fraction of a second, or it could take days, depending on the event. But only after stopping to reflect on the situation can you properly navigate through the simultaneously occurring M. C. Escher "steps" of act, adjust, and communicate.

While I was in college, I had the opportunity in the summer

of my sophomore year to sail a forty-six-foot Morgan Ketch sailboat up and down the Eastern Seaboard with some fellow navy ROTC midshipmen. One night, I was in a famous sailors' bar in Annapolis, surrounded by a bunch of old salty and crusty sailors. I started chatting with one who must have been in his eighties. He was happy to share maritime stories and pass along advice to a young mariner like myself. I was happy to listen.

"One thing all you young bucks do," he told me, "is act too fast when the shit hits the fan. When I have a problem on the boat, do you know what the first thing is I do? I go below deck and pour myself a glass of wine. And I sit and drink that glass of wine and think about the problem. And you know what? More than half the time, when I come back up, the problem has resolved itself."

While there is no time in a firefight to have a glass of wine, what that sailor said stuck with me for my whole career. I knew that before any action, I needed to take a moment to appreciate what was going on around me, even if it was only for a couple of heartbeats. In a firefight, you must identify the direction of fire. Size of the enemy force. What weapons do they have? Then you must take your own resources into account. What's the terrain? What weapons and personnel do you have at your disposal? Do you have air support? Your brain acts like a computer, running internal algorithms by taking in whatever data points are available. Give it a chance to do what it's built to do. Only then can you shoot back or act effectively.

Naturally, there are different degrees of chaotic events, meaning our response should be equally calculated. "Shooting" meant something different when we received the intel than it did when we received actual incoming fire. How we moved was not the same when the convoy traveled across secure terrain as it was when we cleared the hospital. And our communication differed greatly from planning the mission to deciding how to breach the hospital gates. Above everything, you must be nimble in how you shoot, move, and communicate, and you must apply the correct amount of intensity for each scenario.

Let's take changing companies or careers. How do you shoot, move, and communicate when presented with this (relatively) chaotic event? First, you need to take stock of not only what's happening to you but what's happening around you. Look at the situation from both macro and micro perspectives. What is the trajectory of the overall economy? Of your field or sector? What is your personal financial situation? How long can you afford to job hunt? Are jobs available in the geographic area you are in? Is a move possible or advantageous? What are your priorities? Rank them: money, location, job type, lifestyle, changing the kids' schools. These are just a few of the questions you need to begin asking yourself and your family. You won't have perfect answers to them all, but the simple act of considering them will better prepare you to act in an advantageous manner.

As you consciously focus on appreciating the environment you suddenly find yourself a part of, you'll also need to start taking action depending on the factors presented. Applying for jobs, going to interviews, putting the house up for sale, getting additional education for a new career: these could all be potential activities directing you to new, stable territory. Be keen to observe what comes out of those actions, subsequently adjusting to keep you moving on a general azimuth toward your ultimate goals.

As you act and adjust, the communication piece must be happening in parallel. You should be reaching out to people you trust—family, business associates, mentors, friends—and having a conversation with them about the questions posed above. Network. It's difficult for an individual to see all their options and weigh pros and cons on their own. Having an open conversation helps make connections and opens our eyes to possibilities that would otherwise elude us.

To complicate things further, these actions don't always happen step by step or in a vacuum. Subsequent decisions must be fluid. Rather than occurring linearly, each step is circular, like a pinwheel. Each decision and action impacts the next. Don't think of shoot, move, and communicate as tasks to check off in a specific order; think of it more like a Venn diagram of simultaneously occurring events. Each one impacts the other and shapes what happens within the system. Constant iteration and reevaluation of your actions is essential.

Air force colonel John Boyd illustrated this concept in the '70s with something he called the OODA loop, a decision-making process designed to help fighter pilots organize their thoughts and actions in the midst of an airborne dogfight. His observe, orient, decide, and act loop assigns a formula and specific actions to the thought process we should conduct when presented with an adversarial situation. It has been applied to not only tactical, operational, and strategic decision-making in war but also in a variety of domains, from business to sports. Ultimately, Boyd's OODA loop prioritizes agility over power. If you can act and adjust more quickly than the adversary, Boyd surmises that you will win the contest. The goal is to get inside the decision loop of your adversary. The "think, act, adjust, and communicate" loop isn't just about getting inside the loop of an adversary but provides a heuristic for confronting complex situations.

When you graduate from BUD/S and make it to the SEAL Teams, that's when advanced training begins. I began STT, or SEAL Tactical Training (now called SQT, SEAL Qualification Training), shortly after getting assigned to my first SEAL Team. One of the first things you do there are immediate action drills, or IADs. Basically, they're designed to teach you to tactically shoot, move, and communicate.

IADs adhere to the crawl, walk, then run philosophy, which I'll discuss in more depth in a later chapter. In the beginning, the drills are pretty simple: You start with a small group in an open field and add simulated enemy contact. You learn how to provide covering fire so everyone can maneuver while communicating which direction to go. You roll left, roll right, leapfrog back, center peel, and so on, ensuring everyone is on the same page.

Then it gets more complex. You have to start reading the terrain and considering movements three, four, five steps ahead. Then the instructors start piling on more people, adding different elements like smoke and flash grenades and simulated enemy contact from different directions. Then it's a full platoon maneuvering in the woods. You have trees and ditches and streams to contend with. Then we do it at night. Your methods have to advance with the complexity. Where is the terrain advantageous? How do I outflank the enemy? How can I break contact with the enemy? How can I improve my communication?

It's the same in the civilian world. You must take into account the dynamic situation you are operating in, in your business and personal life. What is the "terrain" of the environment? Open your aperture to see all the hills, valleys, trees, ditches, and streams impacting your environment. Which ones can be used to your advantage, and which are detriments to where you want to go? As you navigate unexpected events in your life or business, keep the "think" portion—or Boyd's "observe" portion—at the forefront of your mind. In life and business, the terrain is always changing. This is where it gets tricky: your actions can actually change the terrain, meaning you must constantly think and adjust. Remember, the process is not static; it's a dynamic loop.

As with the career change example, if you choose to use your resources to move to a new city or town that may appear to have more opportunities in your field, you no longer have those resources to pursue additional education in your field. This isn't good or bad; it just is. Every decision you make has an impact on the terrain, which is why you need to be continuously thinking and observing.

That's not to say mistakes aren't made. When they are, they should be used as learning opportunities. In our IAD drills, when we'd screw up, the instructors would stop the drill and show us where we went wrong. Maybe someone missed a piece of cover they could have used. Maybe we maneuvered in one direction, but if we had gone the other way, we could have found cover and concealment in five moves instead of fifteen. It gives you a real appreciation for the environment and how to best utilize it. Like anything, it takes lots of practice, with feedback and hard work.

Communication was paramount during these drills. We were using live bullets. If you turned and ran the wrong way, you could easily have been shot. Our communication came in many forms: it might have been verbal commands via radio or yelling over the gunfire. We also relied on nonverbal communication, like hand signals and even our teammates' body language to indicate intent. Whatever the method, we constantly communicated to move the unit as a single entity with the common purpose of gaining an advantage over the enemy. Sometimes it was to disengage the enemy to fight another day. Our definition of "winning" could vary by scenario.

It's the same in business, no matter the industry. If you have a business that involves more pieces than just you, you must be constantly communicating with your team to ensure everyone is moving in the same direction and don't inadvertently cross purposes. When entities are disconnected from the overall goals of the larger organization, that organization will suffer. You may pay the price in revenue, profits, or talent retention and acquisition, but you will pay a price.

Blockbuster Video failed to appreciate the complexity of their environment by not adapting (or noticing) a disruptive competitor. That lack of nimbleness ultimately put them out of business (except for one remaining store in Oregon).

When Netflix starting mailing DVDs directly to customers and eliminating the need for brick-and-mortar stores, Blockbuster discounted that model. By the time they began offering their movies through the mail, Netflix had adjusted again by offering content online, through streaming. Once again, Blockbuster failed to take inventory of the landscape, and by the time Netflix started producing original content, Blockbuster was two steps behind. Now "Netflix and chill" is as much a part of our society as Friday evening trips to the video store once were. If you can't shoot, move, and communicate, you risk losing everything.

The coronavirus pandemic is the type of disorderly situation that cries out for us to apply think, act, adjust, and communicate. Our decisions addressing the virus will have a long-lasting impact on our lives as well as generations to come. This is not an attempt to judge the actions taken to address the virus; that is a debate for another time. What is not open for debate is that the terrain has been altered and will continue to constantly change in the future. Now is the time to utilize this maxim. Communication needs to equally account for receiving and transmitting information. Seek it out and digest it with a critical eye. Take action, and take advantage. Look into low-interest financing for your business. Take the opportunity to cut nonessentials that may have been holding you back. Explore new ways of communicating with others, both in your business and in your life. Begin by taking informed, thoughtful action. Then be prepared to sense what is happening in the environment and adjust to take advantage of the opportunities or address the subsequent alterations in the landscape. Right now, possibly more than at any other time in recent history, failing to think, act, adjust, and communicate can lead to disaster.

On the other hand, if you embrace and accept the idea that the terrain has changed and the future—while uncertain—is full of opportunity, you can thrive in disorderly times.

4

SPEED, SURPRISE, AND VIOLENCE OF ACTION

When coalition forces invaded Iraq in 2003, Saddam (now Baghdad) International Airport quickly proved itself to be the best defended and most strategic Iraqi position of the entire war. The US Army's First Brigade, Third Infantry Division took the airport down in early April after a fierce fight, allowing it to become the key hub for the US logistics machine for the next seven or eight years.

My team flew into Baghdad International just after First Brigade repelled a major counterattack by Iraqi forces. Our C-130 Hercules pilots were forced to make a combat approach and got us on the ground safely under pretty heavy fire. We immediately got our bearings and set up for the long haul, as we would use the airport as our main base of operations for the remainder of our time in country. Soon my squadron began running missions into Baghdad and beyond, working our way through the "deck of cards" depicting the most-wanted men in Saddam Hussein's regime.

After meeting with a semitrusted source, we believed we had good intelligence on the location of one of those high-ranking bad guys. This guy knew he was being hunted by US forces and was on edge, constantly moving locations with a large contingent of bodyguards. The intelligence was fresh, but we didn't know how long it would be good for. We needed to go after him quickly, and we expected a fight.

We sent the source in with an advance reconnaissance team to ID the exact location of the target house in downtown Baghdad. My team stayed well back while the advance team scouted the route, everyone riding in normal-looking sedans to blend in with the population and ensure we maintained the element of surprise when we launched on the target.

Once the source confirmed location and target, we hit the compound hard. While earlier we had stayed back, out of sight, everyone now moved in as quickly and decisively as possible, covering the target building on all sides. My team stacked against the exterior wall while Little Bird MH-6 helicopters moved in to provide overhead sniper support. We explosively breached the outer wall and rear gates simultaneously while other teammates were boosted onto the wall and took out the external security. Before the smoke and debris from the multiple explosive breach points had settled, our guys were already in the house, giving the enemy no time to respond. Within seconds, we had located the main target, still in bed in his underwear, trying to reach a pistol in the nightstand. We took him down without a fight. During the entire operation, we only fired a few rounds, receiving no return fire from the target or his security. Mission success, and it was because we adhered to our maxims.

We took advantage of timing, both strategically and tactically. We knew we had a small window to complete the mission but still ensured we hit the objective late at night when the target would be less active and we could utilize our technological superiority. There was constant communication during the entire operation as we organized all the elements—the advance recon, snipers, multiple entry assault teams, and external security—into a unified front that shot and moved through the target from start to finish. Because of that communication and coordination, with everyone acting and adapting, we were able to move with an incredible amount of speed and force to retain the element of surprise. Then, once we began the assault, everyone moved with total commitment and dedication. Considering and executing those steps and activities gave us the greatest odds of success.

And that's what it is about: stacking the deck in your favor. It's important to realize that even when you do everything right, success is not guaranteed in a complex, dynamic, and ambiguous world. Using these maxims only turns the odds of a favorable outcome in your favor. If anyone says they can guarantee you success, they're full of it.

In the previous chapter, we learned how shooting, moving, and communicating properly can help bring order to chaos. Speed, surprise, and violence of action do the opposite. While this maxim is not beneficial in every scenario, the key to properly utilizing it is knowing *when* to. These tactics should be deployed when going on the offensive, when you need to act proactively to keep the enemy (or competition) off balance and on their heels.

It should be obvious that none of these maxims stand up as universal laws that apply to every situation. You must use your best judgment, applying where appropriate. For example, if my team was out on a reconnaissance mission, watching a target to gather information that might be of use later, speed, surprise, and violence of action would definitely *not* be appropriate. In fact, it would pretty much be the exact opposite. Deliberate and concealed movement and action. We would want to stay hidden and slip in and out without being detected. Speed, surprise, and violence of action would be counterproductive in such an operation.

In the civilian world, speed, surprise, and violence of action translate to velocity, creativity, and commitment. The tactics and goals are the same as the Navy SEAL application but are articulated differently for noncombat use. Like in the SEAL Teams, these steps should be deployed when the situation calls for proactive action on your terms.

In the SEAL Teams, we obviously use speed to our advantage in many different ways. We're able to swiftly create mission plans, move to and through a target quickly, and cover lots of ground in short periods of time. Think back to Boyd's OODA loop or the maxim of shoot and move (act and adapt): if we can move faster than the adversary can orient itself and act, we have the advantage. We stay one step ahead. Whether it's fast-roping or assaulting a target, once the action starts, you commit and execute with as much speed as your ability allows.

However, "speed" is really a bit of a misnomer. When done

correctly, it's *velocity* that we're utilizing. Speed can certainly be a competitive advantage in both military and nonmilitary usage, but velocity is what you want to focus on. We must ensure those quick movements are leading us in a positive direction, moving as swiftly as possible while remaining in control and toward a common goal.

Speed is simply a scalar quantity for the rate at which an object covers a distance. Speed is direction ignorant. Think of driving from New York to California: going one hundred miles per hour headed north isn't going to get you there faster than going fifty-five miles per hour west. What you need to achieve your goal is velocity. It's a vector quantity, meaning it measures how much something has moved from its original position.

You can also think of speed versus velocity as jogging in place. You can move your feet really fast (speed), but you're going nowhere (no vector component = no velocity). That's what you want to avoid: confusing rapid motion or speed with velocity and progress toward the end goal. This is a common error in the business world and bureaucratic institutions like government. We often confuse being "busy" or doing things with actual productivity. Often those activities are not changing our position. Real improvement requires velocity.

I've watched businesses and government entities over my entire career do lots of things in an effort to move themselves forward. Meeting after meeting, presentations, sales calls, reorganizations, reports, and so on. Those activities may be moving the organization, but are they leading them in the right direction? Lots of activity may just be speed; a vector check may determine that your business, organization, or life is moving without a directional component toward that favorable future we all are seeking.

While this standard does seem to be changing, many people still measure their productivity by how many hours they work, relating more time at the office with more productivity. But that doesn't necessarily equal progress. Stop and take a minute to evaluate your activities and ask if they are really helping move you in a deliberate and favorable direction. If your actions do not line up with an intentional vector, at best you are standing still; at worst, the direction you are moving may be random or even opposite to where you need to be going.

When I was in Afghanistan on my second roll into country, it was becoming apparent to me and many of my fellow SEALs that we were doing a lot of things (speed), but there was no real strategy getting us anywhere (velocity). We attended lots of video conferences, held lots of meetings, produced lots of briefings, went on a lot of patrols, and hit a lot of targets, working day and night, but to what end? The strategic direction was never articulated to me and my circle. How could we move toward a common goal if we didn't know what direction we were supposed to be moving in? It was activity for activity's sake. Short-term thinking. We were doing a lot but not getting anywhere. As a result, nineteen years into the war in Afghanistan, we find ourselves no better off (and arguably worse) than just after 9/11.

About halfway through that deployment, I was living at a safe house in downtown Kabul with a few other SEALs, helping coordinate operations throughout the country. General McChrystal had just taken over as the commanding general of the joint task force that we fell under, and he wanted to up the tempo of operations. He sent one of his deputies to the various units around the country, letting everyone know what the new directive was. When this deputy, an air force brigadier general, came to visit us, four or five of us sat down with him to listen to how General McChrystal was going to redline the force and run operations at a breakneck pace. What that meant in practical terms was that he wanted to conduct more operations. More patrols, more target assaults, more of everything we had already been doing. The strategy was just more of the same. More speed, no strategic direction. He told us that if anyone couldn't keep up, then they needed to get off the team.

Without going into a full analysis of this general's willful ignorance of his audience (not one guy seated with him had fewer than ten years operating in the SEAL Teams, and all had done at least three combat deployments) or his poor leadership skills, needless to say, his message was ill received. One of my guys, a particularly seasoned senior chief whom I had learned a ton from and always relied on, a man who normally held his tongue, spoke up.

He looked at the general and said, "First of all...sir...I know it's your first time in country, but we *have* been running the car at redline RPMs. Second, while we don't mind running the car at redline RPMs, it's wearing us out because you guys don't have the car in gear. Do your job and we'll do ours."

Our leadership's job was to develop a coherent strategy that moved us toward an achievable and favorable goal. Then they needed to communicate that strategy so that everyone was moving on the same vector. Finally, our progress would have to be evaluated on that directional component so we could adapt our actions as necessary or change the vector component if we got too far off track. But they weren't doing that. If you can't articulate clearly where you are trying to go, it becomes impossible to measure your progress or reroute yourself if you get bounced from the path.

My senior chief's message might not have landed, but he was right. The general simply stared back at him, dumbfounded, incredulous that someone dared question the "new strategy" (it was neither of those things) when we just wanted to understand the direction we were moving in to better align our efforts. But the general never took the time to consider what we were telling him. His metrics for success were based on activity—speed, rather than progress toward a goal, or velocity. They say the definition of insanity is continuing to do the same thing over and over and expecting different results. That's what we were doing in Afghanistan.

Not only was a focused direction lacking in the general's plan, so too was any semblance of surprise or, for our purposes here, creativity. We weren't trying anything *different*. Tactically, at ground level, we still leaned heavily on surprise and creativity to complete missions. But from a high-level strategic viewpoint, that just wasn't the case. A classic case of winning the battle but losing the war.

Often there are micro and macro applications to these maxims. In this case, we, the operators on the ground, were still crafting our plans, tactics, and operations to catch the enemy off guard by using surprise and creativity, from how we got to a target to when we would get there to how we conducted our actions once on site. We could come from the sea, air, or land, through a window, door, wall, or ceiling, during the day or during the night—whatever was least expected. We moved fast, focusing on direction and velocity rather than only blunt speed, and we took into account surprise and creativity. Unfortunately, that just wasn't the case for our leadership's high-level strategy in Afghanistan.

Once you understand the need for creativity, you'll have to execute on it. To start with, you must be willing to intellectually explore new and different options. You'll have to allow yourself to wander outside the constraints of what has been done before. Oftentimes creative solutions are counterintuitive or even seem unrealistic, but only by getting out of your comfort zone can you fully act and take advantage of surprise and creativity.

Then the question becomes, How do I come up with a "surprise" action? It's easy to take the familiar path, but again, it's not going to lead you anywhere new. This is about creating something rather than improving on something that already exists. To come up with an innovative solution, you must first open your aperture to explore options that you might not immediately consider in the realm of the possible. You need to look to the extremes.

Take Elon Musk, for example. As of the writing of this book, he is the CEO of Tesla, cofounder of Solar City and Zip2, founder of X.com (later PayPal), and CEO and CTO of SpaceX. This guy knows how to think outside of the box. He certainly does not follow the status quo or allow his vision to be limited to what's already been done. Tesla is the manifestation of his dream for electric and self-driving cars and is just the tip of the iceberg. His companies are digging holes and tunnels under Los Angeles as potential ways to alleviate traffic. He is building reusable rockets to bring down the cost and increase the efficiency and frequency of space travel, with a goal of becoming an interplanetary species. To alleviate the world's dependence on fossil fuels, Musk is working to mass-produce solar panels. Whether or not you agree with the directions or motivations of Musk, his creativity is inarguable. Not all his possibilities will be realized, and his direction component is sure to change as he acts and adapts, but he definitely is not content with just keeping with the status quo.

It's important to openly ideate and not prejudge your ideas before they even see the light of day. As adults, we often negate things just because they are different or haven't been done before. Kids don't do that. They see the possibilities instead of probabilities, suspending judgment. Usually it's an adult who ends up telling them they can't do it. If you say, "I could never do that," then you're right; you can't and won't. But if you consider what is in the realm of possibility and explore those ideas, you just might find a solution or strategy you never considered before. Don't be afraid to consider the potential rather than the likelihood of success. Thinking in these terms will help foster creativity and innovation.

A good exercise to help suspend prejudgment is called the wishing drill. Without focusing on what can actually be done, write down ten wishes. They could be in your personal or professional life, and the likelihood of them coming true is unimportant. Then explore two or three of them intellectually to gauge what is in the realm of possibility. Brainstorm how they could be achieved. Don't limit yourself to what you believe is probable or how something has been done before. Forget about your resources for a minute, and explore how you would go about making your wishes come true if you had no constraints.

You will resist this exercise. "Pie-in-the-sky-type stuff," you'll say. I *do* have constraints on money, time, and so forth. Ignore all that. I'm not saying that you will definitely be able to achieve those wishes, but by opening the creative aperture and exploring the possibilities, you will discover new paths and ways of executing that you never would have found if you were simply bound to what you believed was possible. Remember, this is an intellectual exploration exercise designed to boost creativity. It's not necessarily meant to be implemented; it is simply a tool for helping you drop the baggage of constraints that may be preventing you from finding new ways to achieve your goals. Remember, if you only go with what's known and what's been done before, you'll end up in the same spot.

To further assist you to push through constraints and explore what may be subconsciously or inadvertently holding you back, use another intellectual exercise called the assumption drill. In my consultancy business, Xundis Global, we often use this in our workshops, to great success.

Every industry, domain, or functional area has assumptions associated with it. Spend a few minutes to generate ten assumptions associated with your field. Pick two or three, and begin your inquiry. Where did the assumptions originate from? Has the environment changed? Are the assumptions still valid? Often we find that some of the "facts" are simply assumptions that have been passed on. Their origins can be obscured by the passage of time. Our world is dynamic, not static. Some assumptions that were valid at one time no longer are because the environment and world around us have changed. Likewise, so must our assumptions about navigating that world. Questioning assumptions will open a whole new world of possibilities for your business and your life.

We are constantly exploring and innovating in special operations. We aren't satisfied with conceding, "No, that's not possible." We identify problems that need to be solved and attempt atypical solutions. For example, we wanted to have military working dogs on target with us during combat operations. They can sniff out people and explosives and attack the enemy when needed. But we were limited in how we could get dogs on a target. The military had experimented parachuting with dogs as early as World War I, and it was done in Vietnam in the 1960s from static-line parachutes at relatively low altitudes. While it had been done before, it hadn't been with the precision or extreme conditions that we would expose them to.

We suspended judgment and asked, "Could we strap a dog to our chest and free-fall parachute in from high altitudes?" It was as simple as answering, "Sure, let's try that," and then figuring out how to make it work. We didn't just instantly discount the idea because it sounded hard or hadn't been done before. It took trial and error, but we made it work. Without going into specifics, we figured out (and are constantly improving) how to strap the dogs in, protect their eyes, protect ourselves from their teeth, get them oxygen, and train them to get comfortable with the unnatural act of leaping out of an airplane. Now dogs are intertwined with every special operations group and are basically trained parachutists that can make many different types of jumps with their handlers, ███████████████████████████ ██ ████████████. The creativity in making this work opened up a plethora of other possibilities and options for special operations forces.

Trial and error are OK. Failing is OK, as long as you learn from it. At some point, if you try, you will fail. It's what you do after that matters. You need to get up, reflect on what happened, and learn. If you make the same mistake twice or fail in the same way, you haven't learned. It takes work; creativity doesn't happen in a single stroke of brilliance. Mozart didn't sit down and write his greatest symphonies in a single afternoon. His painstaking process included crafting drafts and fragments, sketching out the composition in pieces. It took many iterations and tweaks before having the complete works we know today. Remember, behind every successful endeavor are dozens of failed attempts and corrections. There are plenty of clichés and quotes about failure, most following the same theme: Try. Fail. Learn. Try again.

One of my favorites is from Denis Waitely, author of *The Psychology of Winning*: "Failure should be our teacher, not our undertaker. Failure is delay, not defeat. It is a temporary detour, not a dead end. Failure is something we can avoid only by saying nothing, doing nothing, and being nothing."

The final part of this maxim, "violence of action," clearly doesn't translate to many fields outside of special operations. In societal terms, it translates to "commitment to action" rather than "violence of action." It means you must have a complete and full commitment to whatever action you are undertaking in order to have any chance at success. Once the decision has been made to do anything—start a new company, write a book, get in shape—you must fully and completely execute with 100 percent effort and dedication if you want to succeed. Nothing less.

One of the surest ways to get hurt in sports is to give a half-assed effort. It's the same in war. Hesitating or not fully committing in combat can get you or a teammate killed. Not fully committing in your professional or personal life can have a proportionately devastating effect.

A common trait found among widely successful people is a profound passion for what they do. Commitment becomes easier when it's organic, sacrifice and effort more palatable when it's for something that you truly love.

In BUD/S, the second I heard a guy mention a "plan B," I knew he was done for. You'd hear someone say, "If this doesn't work out, I can always go back to being a diver or go to the special boat teams," or, "This is really hard on my family. I'm not sure that this lifestyle is fair to them," and invariably, those guys would be gone before you knew it. As soon as they acknowledged doubt and identified a plan B, that warm shower and eight hours of sleep seemed pretty appealing.

It boiled down to their passion and commitment. They either never asked themselves, "How badly do I really want it?" or more likely, they didn't allow for an honest answer. When tackling a new endeavor, that simple question, answered genuinely, is a great predictor of success and failure. It's simple to find and take an alternate route when you aren't passionate about the activity. The guys in BUD/S who do make it are the ones who want it so badly they'll die before quitting. Only passion and full commitment can motivate you to do whatever it takes to win.

That's why you hear so many success stories about the people who quit their jobs, sold all their belongings, and started their own business. That's showing a commitment and willingness to sacrifice everything in order to succeed. They left no room for failure on the grand scale. No plan B. They were willing to go down with the ship, but they had a plan and direction to keep it afloat.

That isn't to say that full commitment is a guarantee of success. It's not, nor are these other lessons. But without them, there's a pretty good guarantee of failure.

Most people know the story of Amazon. When Jeff Bezos started the online retailer in 1995, it only sold books. For the first several years, it didn't turn a profit. But Bezos always had a long-term plan in place to become more than a bookseller, the vision to move that plan forward, and the commitment to execute it.

Bezos utilized each part of velocity, creativity, and commitment to perfection, similar to how we do in the SEAL Teams. If he had been lacking in one part, more than likely we wouldn't be able to order Rudolph socks from our phones on December 23 and wear them to a Christmas Eve party.

Velocity or direction without creativity will get you moving, but most likely with the rest of the crowd, simply following the status quo. Creativity without direction or purpose will leave you on a random walk. It may seem rewarding, but where and when you end up will be completely random. Velocity and creativity without commitment will find you lost and giving up before you really get started. All three parts have to be working in conjunction in order for you to reach your full potential.

5

GET OFF THE X

The kill zone in an ambush is either a really good spot—if you're the one picking it—or a really bad one—if you're stuck on it. We call it the "X," and if our team finds themselves in such a position, we maneuver as quickly and violently as possible to reach a more advantageous fighting position. While it sounds like an easy concept, it's not as straightforward as it seems.

"Getting off the X" is a fundamental concept in the SEAL Teams and something we constantly train on. The idea is that if we get ambushed, we innately patrol through that contact to expertly and adroitly get off the X. We don't want to fight on the enemy's terms, and we certainly don't want to be stuck where they have the advantage. But sometimes, with a fierce and prepared opponent, getting stuck on the X is an unavoidable hazard.

Remember, the enemy gets a say. I had a close friend and teammate killed when guys in my squadron were ambushed and found themselves in a kill zone in Afghanistan in August of 2003. I was in Kabul providing support for the mission and heard everything go down on the radio. We had been following the operation's progress closely and listening to each checkpoint call, so I knew approximately where our guys were when the team leader's next update came in. His report of "troops in contact" crackled over the radio, making my heart skip a beat.

The squadron was patrolling in the Paktika province, a lawless area on the Pakistani border where al-Qaeda and the Taliban ran rampant. It had already been a long couple of days away from the forward operating base and under the constant threat of ambush when incoming fire began impacting their convoy.

The enemy had picked the perfect spot for their ambush: the roads (a loose term) in that area were just rutted dirt and mud, lined by steep cliffs that rose hundreds of feet above. A perfect kill zone. Anytime we traveled through those areas, I would feel the hair stand up on the back of my neck and wanted to hold my breath. On this day, the enemy was waiting, and they rained down AK-47 and RPG fire on the patrol from high atop the cliff walls. They had the high ground and were essentially invisible, making effective return fire next to impossible. Our team would have to get out of the kill zone—off the X—as quickly as possible.

We heard most of the battle on the radio but couldn't be sure exactly what was happening in between updates. We didn't want to interfere, so we didn't chime in, just waited, doing what we could to help from 150 miles away. Early on, the team leader requested aerial support, so we knew the battle was raging. Then a call of "two friendlies wounded" came across the net. We started working on a medevac helicopter. The team's next update delivered the phrase we never wanted to hear: "One Sierra expectant." It meant one of our SEALs was not expected to make it.

The team leader did everything right that day. He quickly turned chaos into order, employing the concepts of shoot, move, and communicate to get the team through the kill zone and off the X. He began directing return fire at the enemy positions, got the vehicles moving, and recovered the wounded, all while communicating with overhead air support and higher headquarters. But in such a well-planned kill zone, casualties were almost inevitable.

For the most part, our guys couldn't see where the fire was coming from. The enemy was able to poke their weapons over the cliff ledges and spray deadly rounds down at our convoy. The team knew the priority was to get off the X, and within minutes, despite the extremely chaotic situation, they were able to maneuver through the ambush and make their way to a relatively safe area. They established a helicopter landing zone, allowing a medevac to land and get the wounded out and treated as quickly as possible. Every one of the vehicles was riddled with bullet holes, leaving some inoperable. They had two wounded SEALs, including the one who would succumb to his injuries at a hospital in Bagram.

It was an incomprehensible and devastating loss of a friend, teammate, father, husband, brother, and son, but the casualties could have been magnified many times over had the team frozen and remained on the X.

Events ambush us in life and business all the time: A new competitor takes market share. You get sued. Sales are down. The family relocates. A loved one dies. There's no avoiding the ambushes of life. What is important is how you respond to them. How you get off the X and into a better position that will allow you to win the event. We've dealt with tactics in previous chapters that you can use to deal with these events, and in this chapter we'll further explore how to turn an ambush into an advantage.

First and foremost, you cannot allow yourself to freeze. You must immediately move and take action. We already know that the first thing to do when presented with a chaotic event is to think or, in Boyd's terms, orient yourself. That must be immediately followed by decisive action.

Unfortunately, an all-too-common event requiring immediate action in a literal kill zone is becoming more and more prevalent in this country: mass shootings. The worst thing a person can do if they find themselves in such a scenario is to freeze. Depending on the situation and resources available, you may find yourself implementing any of the maxims we've already outlined: reinforcing the importance of considering when to move, shoot, or act; when to communicate; and where and how to do so, with full commitment to getting off the X.

Your first decision is whether to run, hide, or fight. Those are your only three options, and you must use the data points provided to choose the right action. Be aware of ingress and egress points at your location, and if you can run, do so. If you can't, hide. Take either cover or concealment, but understand the difference between the two. *Concealment* hides you from sight, but only *cover* protects you from bullets. A wooden door is concealment, not cover. Ideally, you'd like to find cover. If none is available and you can't run, then you must fight to your last breath. Above all, never stop trying to get off the X and to a position that levels the playing field or, better yet, tilts it in your favor.

Sometimes the X isn't a physical ambush point created by an

enemy, adversary, competitor, or disruptive event. It isn't always something tangible. Often the X is something we create ourselves, in our own minds. It's target fixation.

For our entire lives, we've been taught to "keep our eye on the prize" and focus on our goals. And certainly, being able to identify an objective and go after it is an important element of success. But we run the risk of ignoring potentially disastrous by-products or windows of opportunity along the way when we get fixated *only* on that end goal without taking other side effects into account. There's a real danger of getting attached to a linear focus. Sometimes you can't see the forest for the trees and find yourself stuck on an X of your own making.

A company exists to make profits for the owners, employees, and shareholders. That's obvious. But when a fixation on those profits supersedes everything else the company stands for—employee satisfaction, customer service, ethics, legality, and reputation—it can come at a great cost.

This is exactly what happened to Wells Fargo a few years ago. The huge banking institution suffered an account fraud scandal that it may never fully recover from. They got stuck on the X of revenue over all else and lost sight of what it meant to run an effective, moral, and ethical company, costing them billions of dollars and thousands of customers.

It began with the common practice of cross-selling. Basically, they encouraged existing customers to open additional accounts with them. Those who had checking accounts were given savings accounts. Mortgage holders were offered investment accounts and credit lines. New credit cards and insurance policies were opened. The practice was so heavily encouraged, with such outrageous quotas set by management, that employees began to open new accounts for customers without their knowledge or approval. They began charging fees for many of these products that customers had never signed up for. Employees moved money from account to account without customer knowledge. Millions of new lines were opened, and customers were charged unapproved fees for products ranging from renters insurance to life insurance. Soon the *Wall Street Journal* and *Los Angeles Times* got wind of the fraud and wrote articles about the unscrupulous company practices, leading to a government investigation. Even with that scrutiny, Wells Fargo did not immediately take steps to stop the pressure on branches and employees to fill these quotas. They were still stuck on the X of revenue.

When the government concluded its investigation, they hit Wells Fargo with over a billion dollars in fines. It cost the CEO his job and delivered a hit to the company's reputation that they will be spending years to repair, if it ever can be. Wells Fargo put themselves in a kill zone of their own making with their fixation on a single objective.

The thing about a self-inflicted kill zone is that you might not even realize you've placed yourself in one. But often when we find ourselves in the everyday ruts of life, it's because we've unwittingly put ourselves there. A dieter focused on losing those last ten pounds keeps doing the same workout every morning. A wife unhappy in her marriage doesn't communicate her issues to her husband. A worker stuck at a dead-end job doesn't summon the drive to find a better situation. They keep doing the same things and expecting different results. There's no creativity or movement, keeping each of them stuck on their own X.

If you've plateaued on an exercise program, you need to shock the system. Instead of lifting low weights with high reps, do the opposite. If you've been running every morning, try swimming. Not happy with your job? What are you doing about it? Do you need to go back to school? Move? Network? Getting up every morning and going to the same office you despise is not moving you toward progress.

Unhappy marriage? That doesn't mean to try a side relationship with someone else. Do something to spice up the marriage. Schedule date nights, leave love notes, attend couples' therapy. These are all movements to get you into a better fighting position.

We all possess blinders that predispose us to harboring our own personal Xs. Many of these predilections happen at the subconscious level, meaning oftentimes we aren't even aware they're there. These cognitive biases subconsciously influence us and push us in directions we may think we want to go but aren't necessarily the best path for us. The biases can play with our minds. Sometimes, even when you believe you are making a rational decision, you might not be. Cognitive or psychological biases may lead to missed opportunities, faulty judgment, and poor decision-making.

The first step to countering cognitive blinders and biases is *awareness*. Recognize that the human brain is a complex mechanism and is susceptible to being convinced of things that might not necessarily be true.

Once identified, it's as simple (and as difficult) as seeking out information that discounts your accepted point of view and offers counter data points to disprove it. It's human nature, of course, to do the opposite. Makes sense: we innately want to confirm our thoughts and beliefs to know that our ideas are right and everyone else is wrong. In order to rid ourselves of these blinders and see an unobstructed world, we must fight those preconceived notions. Once again, we must seek the counterintuitive and actively seek to disprove our hypotheses.

If you only watch Fox News, flip the channel to CNN (or vice versa). Observe an issue from multiple perspectives. Seek out a range of source material, and keep an open mind. Apply more weight to the contrary position. We tend to interpret statistics and data in favor of our position and discount the data that counters it. If you support gun control, you read and interpret the statistics to reinforce your position. If you oppose gun control, the same statistics can be construed to support your position. Try viewing an issue from the opposing lens.

In business, think about the hiring process and how it can be impacted by confirmation bias. Do you have a preconceived notion of what the ideal candidate looks like? Would you favor a Harvard graduate over someone coming from a community college? Short hair over long hair? Someone wearing a tie over a polo? Would you ask the candidate different questions if they did or didn't fit the appearance of what you were looking for? How many opportunities have HR departments missed because they were unconsciously influenced by confirmation bias? I would argue that it's quite a lot.

There's also a danger in viewing assumptions and accepted beliefs as facts. We've all been told since childhood that marijuana is bad. Not bad in some instances, not just bad for kids, but outright *bad* in all circumstances, with no redeeming qualities. Historically, that has been an accepted fact and never really disputed by the general populace. But is it accurate? Is it a fact or just an assumption? We're now hearing from the medical community—and society at large—that marijuana might have some strong medicinal qualities and applications. Did society miss out on a potentially safe pain-killing solution for generations due to its cognitive blinders? Maybe.

It's human nature to not question the status quo; it's easier on our brains to not muster the energy to consider alternatives to what we've always accepted. If a widely held principle is what most people believe and is the way it's always been done, then why buck the system? Of course, if everyone adhered to that philosophy, we wouldn't have parachuting dogs or Amazon delivering packages the next day. True innovators are able to see around and through how things are and always have been. They don't get stuck on the Xs of their own prejudices or widely accepted assumptions.

In the 1960s and '70s, it was pretty much universally accepted that democracy and the American way of life were in danger each time Communism took a foothold in another country. Our foreign policy was built around the domino theory and doing everything in our power to stop the spread of Communism. The theory forced us into brutal wars in Korea and Vietnam (as well as skirmishes in other countries), bred the Cold War, cost taxpayers trillions of dollars, and put us on the brink of nuclear holocaust. Was the danger actually there, or did everyone just assume it was? There's no way to answer that now, but the history and direction of our country were undoubtedly changed because of that assumed fact.

The point is, it's always a good idea to question the standard and seek out new information across a diverse spectrum, especially as time goes on. The world, and the truths inherent with it, changes over time. When new events or information comes to light, they have to be added into your calculus.

There's an advantage to playing the devil's advocate, if only to gain a differing point of view. This does not mean that you must accept the contrarian view. But recognizing and acknowledging it will help you confirm or discount the preconceptions you subconsciously harbor. Only then can you get off the X you've created and see what else is out there.

Target fixation can also have physical repercussions. I saw this regularly in the Teams, especially when doing air operations. We would be parachuting to a target or practicing air insertions when guys would succumb to literal target fixation: they'd only concentrate on the drop zone, sometimes miles away, not taking into account the dozens of factors affecting the jump, including teammates in the air around them.

We do all types of jumps in the SEAL Teams, in all types of conditions. High-altitude low-opening (HALO) jumps, high-altitude high-opening (HAHO) jumps, static-line jumps; jumps during the day, during the night, with dogs strapped to us, with a hundred pounds of gear, with oxygen, with boats; single-man jumps, tandem jumps, and then mass jumps of sixty men or more all trying to land on the same drop zone.

When jumping in groups under square parachutes, one method we use to organize the descent and landing is to organize into a stack. These stacks come in staggered at different altitudes, each man ten to twenty feet behind and ten to twenty feet above the guy in front of them. If done properly, it looks like a staircase of parachutes. But if just one guy doesn't have his head on a swivel, or if someone gets out of position, bad things can happen. I've seen guys crash into each other in the air. Parachutes can get tangled, or you can steal someone else's air and cause their parachute to collapse. A guy might not notice another jumper until the last minute, forcing them to suddenly turn to avoid a collision and put them off course.

It happens for a variety of reasons. Getting in the stack and staying in the stack can be difficult. Guys fall at different rates depending on their weight and what they're carrying. They're searching for the drop zone instead of making the adjustments in the air to maintain their position in the stack. Maybe they got off on their initial opening and weren't able to reach the stack.

While the primary focus is landing on that drop zone, in order to do it safely, you have to constantly make the necessary adjustments as you fall, taking into account wind speed, direction, height, situation on the ground, monitoring GPS, your altimeter, and yes, where the other guys are that you're jumping with. If you forget about those things and only focus on the end goal, you risk missing it.

I remember a training mission once when one of my teammates got fixated on lights in the distance, thinking it was the drop zone. He didn't check his compass (we weren't all jumping with GPS systems back then) for the correct bearing and stayed locked on those lights. When he and the guys following him finally landed, they were twenty miles off target.

Twenty of us jumped that night. The first sixteen jumped without incident, pulling our chutes shortly after exiting the aircraft at twenty thousand feet and getting organized into a stack and making our way to the drop zone.

For some reason, this guy, the seventeenth jumper, was delayed, causing him to lose sight of the stack. Once he pulled his chute and oriented himself, he headed toward some lights in the distance that he believed matched up with the drop zone (DZ). The last three jumpers followed him, assuming he was in the stack and behind the lead jumper. A classic case of the blind leading the blind. They were each so confident they were oriented correctly that no one checked their compass.

While in the air, we started doing radio check-ins to make sure everyone was accounted for. Seventeen, eighteen, nineteen, and twenty checked in along with everyone else, so we assumed they were in the stack and good to go. It wasn't until they landed in a strip-mall parking lot that they realized their error. Needless to say, there were some pretty embarrassed jumpers that night who learned some hard lessons about target fixation, making assumptions, and confirmation bias.

It sounds simpler than it is, but if you focus on keeping an eye out for the X, you can avoid it or at least know to navigate it. Watch out for the traps of status quo thinking, confirmation biases, and a long list of other cognitive biases that are constantly at work in our subconscious. Dig in and do some additional research on all the forces at play in your head. Awareness is the first line of defense. Inevitably, however, at some point in your life, you will find yourself on an X of either your own or someone else's creation. When you recognize yourself in that spot, reflect on the maxims in this book, and you will be prepared to act decisively and deliberately to get off the X and out of danger.

6

TWO IS ONE,
ONE IS NONE

Two weeks after Hell Week ended my body was finally getting
back to normal. There had been the expected chafing and raw
sores in most of my crevices, along with coughing up plenty
of red, green, gray, and purple phlegm from smoke grenades,
but all that was pretty standard for post–Hell Week. My feet
were the biggest issue: they had swollen so badly with folliculitis that I couldn't remove my boots the last two days. If I had,
I would never have gotten them back on. In fact, after our class
was secured, they had to cut my laces just to get each boot off,
leaving indentations nearly a quarter inch deep across my feet
and shins.

But Hell Week was now in the past, and as I sat shivering on the
pool deck with the rest of Class 191, twin 80-cubic-foot scuba tanks
on my back, I was ready for BUD/S's second phase: combat diving.

My remaining classmates and I weren't particularly taken aback when one of our instructors, a particularly quirky chief, came out to address us wearing only a red Speedo. It was just getting light out as he stood before us in that tight little bathing suit, holding a cup of coffee and offering a friendly, "What's going on, gents?"

We gave our regular response, a deafening "Hooyah, Chief!"

"Dive phase, huh?" he asked rhetorically, looking us over. "Pretty nice having masks when you're underwater, isn't it?"

"Hooyah, Chief!"

"Yeah, it is. You should really learn to appreciate them. I want to help you. Let's try an evolution that will help you develop an appreciation for those masks."

By now we were all looking at each other, knowing this wasn't going to be good. We awaited further instruction.

"This is going to be awesome, isn't it!" he said, grinning behind his coffee. "Everybody fill up yer masks with water and put 'em on! Now, on your backs. Flutter kicks!"

We all scrambled to fill our masks with the chlorinated pool water before lying on our tanks, raising and lowering our legs while trying our best to breathe from our mouths since the water-filled masks now covered our noses and eyes. If you did try to close your eyes to protect them from the stinging water, you could be sure an instructor would notice pretty quickly and come over and encourage you to keep them open. Overall, it was a pretty miserable evolution.

"This is what happens if you don't have a mask, gents, or don't take care of your mask. It cracks. It fills with water. Your eyes burn. You can't see. Life sucks. Don't we all appreciate our masks even more now?"

"Hooyah, Chief."

That was one of my first lessons in the Navy about "two is one, one is none." "Mask appreciation" taught us in the BUD/S way that when something is important, you can't leave it to chance that it will always function and work properly. Success cannot be dependent upon a single point of failure. Hence the reason we would carry backup masks on dive missions. And infilled to targets on multiple helos. And came up with several mission plans before assaulting an objective. We couldn't leave it to chance that the one "something" we were depending on wouldn't somehow fail.

That attention to redundancy is equally important in the real world. And while it's not rocket science, there is a methodology to what and how you should protect against those single points of failure.

We carried a lot of redundant gear in the SEAL Teams, both individually and as a unit. When every ounce counted, we put a lot of thought into what we took and why. Consider a secondary weapon, for instance. Naturally, we each carried a rifle on every operation, but we had a pistol too, in case something happened to the rifle. Say we ran out of ammo, or it jammed; we still needed to be able to shoot back. Notice we didn't take another rifle; that would have been too cumbersome, and besides, we wanted to vary any backup equipment we carried. It's always nice to have a second, complimentary feature set. There are some instances where a pistol may be preferable to a long gun, especially in extremely tight spaces like tunnels or small hatches on ships. Not only was a pistol protection against the rifle failing, it also offered diversity. The idea is to make your redundant system diverse by filling the primary function and also offering additional capabilities. Whether it's a business plan or a weapon, you don't want your backup susceptible to the same failure point as the primary.

If you're camping, you don't want to bring two lighters with you. If one does fail, there's a good chance that whatever caused the failure will affect the backup as well. Take a box of matches or a flint instead. Seek out similar items with overlapping functions that can be utilized in different environments or situations.

Look at an NFL team: They're allowed to carry fifty-three men on the active roster. They need to be strategic about how they fill that roster and what positions need to be redundant. It's a risk versus reward (or consequence) analysis: Quarterback is the most important position on the team, so it's a good idea to have two or three on the roster. If one goes down, the team would be screwed without a backup. A kicker, not so much. This is where overlapping redundancies come into play, because teams usually carry field goal kickers and punters. Worst case scenario, the remaining kicker can step into the others' role. The rarity of kickers getting injured is also taken into account. Players who can step into multiple positions are particularly valuable to an NFL team. If a lineman can play center, guard, and tackle, they reinforce several positions while only taking up a single roster spot: redundant with multiple capabilities. When building in your own backups in life, it's important to do so strategically.

I always carried two knives with me on ops: one a fixed blade, the other a multitool like a Gerber or Leatherman. Not only did that secondary tool fill the function of my primary knife should it get lost or broken, it provided other features like pliers and wire cutters.

If you're building a home gym, chances are you have limited space and resources; you can't install the same amount of equipment as a fitness center. You have to be smart about what you put in. Sure, you could get by with just an Olympic bar and some bumper plates, but by adding dumbbells, kettlebells, and a pull-up bar, you increase the diversity of available workouts. But you probably wouldn't add a fly machine, a Smith machine, and multiple squat racks. It's an obvious example of intuitively prioritizing redundancies and accounting for diversity.

The reality is, you can't carry or install two of everything. That's why it's so important to identify which things are critical to mission success, then deliberately and strategically choose where you want to enjoy redundancies. Dive masks and weapons were crucial to mission success, hence the concerted effort on abundance. It wasn't feasible to take two pairs of boots or two gas masks or two backpacks on every mission. We live in a resource-constrained environment. As an operator, I was constrained by the amount I could physically carry. Where would I put an extra rucksack?

If your business would completely fail without power or electricity, such as at a data center, you probably should have a generator for backup power. Alternatively, if you use customer relationship management (CRM) software as part of your business, is it worth the time and resources to have an additional one? If you have Salesforce CRM software, it would be ridiculous to invest in a redundant CRM platform.

This formal (or informal) cost benefit analysis is integral in deciding which redundancies to build in and just how redundant they need to be. Most of us back up our computer files and documents to a cloud-solution provider like Dropbox or One

Drive, and our phones to a laptop. If we lose our phone or the computer melts down, we can restore the information from those backups. If you're already taking such precautions, is it necessary to invest further time and money in additional redundancies? Would it be overkill, say, to also download your computer's data each day to a portable hard drive, take it to a bank, and store it in a safety deposit box? I suppose that depends on your appetite for potentially losing the data. For most of us, those extra steps are not necessary or cost and time effective. However, if there are trade secrets or information that would lead to catastrophe if lost, maybe the effort is justified. It's that same risk versus reward (or consequence) calculation as above: What is the burden of the redundancy versus the penalty of a failure while also considering the likelihood of one? In this case, the equation takes into account the time spent transferring the data over to a portable hard drive, plus the time and effort of opening a safety deposit box and driving the hard drive to the bank each day. Then factor in the money spent on the drive and renting the box. Finally, compare those commitments to the chance your other redundancies could fail (like Google Drive or Box) and the repercussions should your data be lost. In the unlikely event those cloud backups fail and you only lose pictures of your dog and your old college term papers, the juice probably isn't worth the squeeze. But if you're dealing with sensitive customer information, then it's probably a good idea to consider a more in-depth backup solution. The additional time and cost to protect that valuable data is marginal compared to the ramifications of losing it.

There are instances when a single point of failure is unavoidable, and it's up to you to decide if that endeavor is worth the risk.

A lot of guys I served with did BASE jumping on their off time. In general, SEALs gravitate toward high-adrenaline hobbies, and if the skydiving and gunfights inherent with our job aren't enough, there are other high-risk activities like motorcycle racing and BASE jumping to keep guys entertained.

BASE jumping was one those activities that I chose not to participate in. The risk of having no redundant system should your primary fail just wasn't worth it to me. Sure, it's fun, but with a single point of failure whose consequence was death, I chose to forgo that activity. Other guys had different equations, and with the same information and operating under the same risks, they did it all the time. Their appetite and calculation of risk versus reward differed from mine, and that's OK.

There are plenty of examples of when redundancy is simply not practical due to availability of resources. We live in a world of constraints and limitations—money, space, and time being the most common impediments. When faced with any of these varying restrictions, choosing a redundancy becomes about recognizing vulnerabilities and mitigating them as much as possible. Sometimes the only mitigation of risk you can achieve is simply awareness, but even that small step will contribute to your resilience.

The body is not a system with much built-in redundancy, and humans are unable to go out and procure extra parts should the need arise. Yet those limitations do not leave us powerless to develop resilience and mitigate risk. A healthy diet and regular physical exercise go a long way toward preserving those single points of failure inherent with our bodies. Even small changes can increase our longevity and quality of life. As the world grapples with coronavirus, studies have shown that something as simple as getting up and going outside for fresh air can help strengthen our immune systems. Other healthy practices like cutting as many refined sugars from your diet as possible, eating moderate portions, and beginning an exercise program can drastically mitigate points of failure.

Anyone who has parachuted before certainly understands the two is one, one is none concept. When you're rocketing toward the ground at 120+ miles per hour, it's sure nice to know that there's a reserve parachute in addition to your main chute. In fact, once you've gotten a couple hundred jumps under your belt, chances are you've had that main chute fail at some point. It could have been because of your body position when you released the parachute, or maybe the chute wasn't folded and packed correctly into the container. But a failure is always a real possibility, and it's important to properly prepare for it.

This is why it's standard practice to have someone else who is certified pack your reserve and inspect your parachute before testing it at twelve thousand feet. Employing another party for additional quality control should be looked at as another redundant measure. Unlike activating the reserve chute, this step takes place *before* jumping. Protecting against single points of failure does not just take place during the activity. It starts with planning.

You must consider where a plan can go wrong—and then protect against it—before ever going out on a mission, starting a new business, or making a personal life decision. Not only must you hedge against points of failure, you should prepare the original item or plan to be as foolproof as possible. That's why we spent so much time prepping and inspecting our gear when I was in the SEAL Teams. It's why you should have multiple people you trust reviewing your business plan or checking out that new house you want to buy. Seek feedback from objective, dispassionate outside observers, and prepare for multiple scenarios. We'll talk about this in a future chapter, but it's like we say in the Teams: the more you sweat in peace, the less you bleed in war. Translation: do as much prework as possible so you are as prepared as possible for whatever goes wrong (because something will).

With proper practice and preparation, you can limit the need for redundancy, but there is no way to eliminate points of failure all together. And that preparation needs to start before a disruptive event occurs.

Understand that any plan with only a single point of failure is destined to find that point. That's why every financial planner talks about diversifying your portfolio. You can't invest in just one financial sector—you have to incorporate equities, bonds, commodities, mutual funds, and cash on hand into a well-rounded plan. Those investments should be reviewed and balanced depending on things like your investment goals (which change as you get closer to retirement), the health of the market, and how you and your advisor see the economy trending.

Plans change. Your environment changes. Equipment and technology improve (or decline). You grow as a person. Your appetite for risk wanes. Or increases. These outside influences mean you must be nimble and creative with your redundancies. What worked yesterday might not work tomorrow. The goal of being well rounded should be used as protection against points of failure in everything you do.

If you are self-employed or an entrepreneur, you understand how important multiple streams of income are. If you're relying on one customer or service to keep you afloat, you're headed for disaster. It's a bad idea to specialize in only one thing or to only sell to one market. Your business should be multifaceted to not only survive but thrive during downturns and unexpected influences. Maybe there is seasonality to your business, sudden competition appears, or a global pandemic demands physical distancing. No matter what the outside pressure is, you must be prepared to adapt with it.

Having been immersed for years in a world of secrecy, I always shunned the idea of social media. I didn't have Facebook, LinkedIn, or Instagram. But my environment has changed. I'm retired and have started down the civilian path, so there is no longer a need to be cloaked in the same shroud of secrecy. I had to change my perception of social media in my new world. Instead of avoiding it, I worked to learn more about it, figuring out the advantages and disadvantages and trying to use it to my benefit. Truth be told, I'm still working on it—change and reinvention are difficult!

IBM is a perfect example of a dexterous company that has been able to reinvent itself time and time again. Since their inception over a hundred years ago, they've sold—as the name, International Business Machines, implies—hardware. They started with tabulation machines, grew into making computers for the government, and, along with Microsoft, were instrumental in the "PC revolution." But when competition in the personal computer market began taking copious amounts of market share, they knew they had to adapt. The market was oversaturated, and they realized that if they kept doing what they had always done, they would be dead in the water. So International Business Machines stopped making machines and started offering technology and consulting services. Recognizing that they had to evolve, they put a plan in place to do so, executed it, and are now thriving under the new model, taking in billions in revenue every year.

IBM's willingness to completely change course and focus on a new revenue stream is a great illustration of having the self-awareness to recognize a single point of failure and the guts to pivot from it. Discovering and admitting to yourself that the primary plan has faults are just as important as implementing redundancies. Recognizing deficiencies should not be looked upon as a negative; rather, planning for disruptions can actually help improve performance and solidify the original plan.

Nassim Taleb is a former Wall Street trader, an author, and a philosopher who focuses on uncertainty, probability, and randomness. His five-volume work on uncertainty, the *Incerto* series, is certainly worth taking the time to read. Two of the core works, *The Black Swan* and *Antifragile*, are particularly adept at appreciating and developing approaches to dealing with uncertainty and randomness.

Taleb's core idea of antifragility is that stressors can help improve performance. Proof that it's important to shock the system so you can properly adapt and flex when it's called for.

All too often nowadays, kids, especially ones who are good athletes, only play one sport, and they do it year-round. The top basketball players quit baseball after Little League to play in travel leagues, while soccer players have indoor games during the winter. But you know what helps football players improve their balance and core strength? Yoga. A right-handed quarterback or pitcher constantly overusing that side of his body is going to experience muscle deterioration and flexibility issues on the left side, especially as he's growing into his body. Something simple like cross-training could eliminate that. Having a narrow focus in anything just means you're reliant on that single point of failure—not a good place to be. We've used the plateauing in an exercise program example before: if you reach your bench-press max, it's a good idea to spend more time working your back or triceps. You need to shock the system.

Businesses with a single employee managing their accounting software or one vendor handling all their printing make themselves vulnerable. What happens if that employee is hit by the proverbial bus? Gets a new job or ends up being dishonest? What if that single vendor raises prices by 20 percent or goes out of business?

When planning a mission, we would always build in multiple contingency plans. We would hit the target from multiple dimensions, diversifying the force. We came in from the front and the back door. We always kept our options open while taking into consideration what could potentially go wrong. Murphy's Law was always lurking around the corner, waiting to grab you when you least expected it.

We were on a multiple-day reconnaissance in the mountains of Kosovo when Murphy made an appearance. We had reviewed the plan multiple times. It was supposed to be a relatively simple mission: monitor a remote road intersection for suspicious vehicle activity and report back so that other forces could intercept the traffic. We chose what we thought was a great position overlooking the road in question. It was extremely difficult to get to, nestled in the rocks on the slope of a steep hill, and provided great cover as well as a good vantage point to see all the vehicle and foot traffic coming in and out of the area.

Within hours of getting into position, a couple of kids who

were following sheep through the woods came over the rocks and walked right into our position. Unbelievable. It was just after dusk—what were the chances they wouldn't have finished herding the sheep by nightfall? What were the chances that the sheep would have wandered near our position? What were the chances that the kids would have followed those animals all the way up the mountain and right into the middle of our position? Apparently really good!

The kids didn't spot us until they were about a foot away from my point man. They nearly walked right on him. The kids had a look of fear and shock when they found themselves inches away from a completely camouflaged figure with only the whites of his eyes showing. We ushered the terrified kids back downhill with the universal hand signal of a finger to the lips to be quiet.

We were compromised and knew we had to move our position before their parents and villagers came looking for them. No problem—we had a contingency plan. We gathered all our gear and sprinted to another mountaintop across a valley a couple of kilometers away. The new position still afforded us a view of the intersections we needed to watch. We were set up a couple hours before dawn and were even able to observe the flashlights and patrols searching the hill we had been on. The mission was still a go, but unfortunately, Murphy wasn't done. Just after dawn, an unexpected thunderstorm cropped up. We spent the next three days in a torrential downpour, covered in clouds and fog, unable to see farther than fifty feet in front of us. It no longer mattered if we were watching the intersection anymore. The roads were so overcome with mudslides that nothing significant moved in or out of the area for at least a week. Even though we had done everything we could to mitigate the risk, with backup plans in place, sometimes circumstances are out of your control.

Of course, at some point you have to stop examining perceived weak links and execute. We couldn't plan indefinitely. Intelligence was usually time sensitive, as opportunities in the real world can be. Often our targets were people. If we waited too long to execute the raid, the target could change locations or shore up defenses. Again, we live in a resource-constrained world. In this case, the resource is time. We only have so much of it, and only so many windows of opportunity. You can't expect to cover all the angles. Top athletes can't play five different sports without their primary sport suffering, and you can't bring five masks with you on a dive. Overplanning leads to paralysis by analysis. Like everything in life, you need to find a balance.

Yeti makes rugged merchandise designed to hold perishables and serve its owner in the outdoors. I just made that synopsis up, because Yeti does a really good job of not pigeonholing itself into a particular market. Or at least they do now. While they built their brand name on a single product category to create the high-end cooler market, they were smart enough to realize they were vulnerable. Which is why they no longer rely on one product to keep them in business. Nor did they get so broad that they lost sight of what their customers relied on them for and what they did well. They don't build computers or sell produce. They found a niche, then strengthened and expanded it. They grew smartly by creating additional, related products that sat firmly in their wheelhouse. They didn't expand so much that they lost sight of who they were. They focused on items like coolers and canisters and bags and blankets and even dog bowls. Disparate items, yes, but still related. As you avoid single points of failure, so can those redundancies overlap. If you're going on a camping trip, Yeti has a great cooler for you. You may also need a portable chair and a hardy sleeping bag; they have you covered. But if you need jumper cables, you're going to have to look elsewhere.

When Yeti started, I'm sure they didn't offer the wide range of products they can now after years in business. That's the reality of a startup: it's harder to be redundant when you're working with fewer resources. Risk is inherent in everything you do, and we know there's no way to eliminate that. Risk is not necessarily a bad thing, as long as it is calculated risk.

If you're a small-business owner, early on you're still largely in survival mode. You might not have the resources to hire a sales-person or someone to manage your accounting software; taking on that risk is simply part of the game. And that's perfectly fine, as long as you understand those risks and take them on knowl-edgeably and not randomly. You can prepare for them. Once you fully understand the risks, then you can appreciate the con-sequences and not be surprised when something breaks.

Some of those risks can be mitigated with a strong support structure. You're always stronger with a team than you are alone. It's good practice to build a network of coworkers, coaches, team-mates, family members, and friends. Bounce ideas off them, especially if they have no skin in the game. You'll get honest feed-back and protections you may have never considered.

Many of the evolutions at BUD/S are designed to strengthen the concept of two is one, one is none. Early on, the concept of a swim buddy was introduced for open-ocean swims, and we were paired with someone who swam at a similar speed. We never went on an ocean swim or conducted a dive without our swim buddy. This ensured someone was always keeping an eye on you and vice versa.

The Pacific Ocean off Coronado, California, is cold, even in the summer. Hypothermia, cramping, and fatigue were real dangers on open-ocean swims. It would have been easy for a single swimmer to go hypothermic or cramp up and slip beneath the water without anyone noticing. Having a swim buddy prevented this from happening. Two is one, one is none.

The same concept was applied to diving and became even more important. So important that we had a six-foot line tethering our wrists together. If your dive rig failed, you could buddy breathe to safety. Two is one, one is none.

If you experienced medical problems like oxygen toxicity and went unconscious, your dive buddy or swim buddy could save your life. We extended this into every aspect of life. When we headed out to the bars or nightclubs, especially in a foreign country, we always made sure that we buddied up. Redundancy. Two of you are more likely to avoid or handle trouble than one.

This is why most special operations selection courses utilize some type of log training. It's a great way to figure out who really wants to be there. You can't hide when you're under a two-hundred-pound log with five or six of your teammates, lugging it through the obstacle course or pushing it overhead while lying in the surf. If you aren't fully putting out, that log isn't going anywhere, and everyone knows exactly who the weak link is. That's the idea: to eliminate known points of failure.

Remember, you're always stronger with others, unless those others amount to weak links and end up dragging you down. Ensure your team and your redundancies are each dependable. Always take into account and prepare against single points of failure.

7

CRAWL, WALK, RUN

It was a beautiful night. The sky was relatively clear, a half-moon hanging over the horizon. Thousands of stars sparkled clearly across the darkness. I glanced out the open rear ramp of the C-17 Globemaster aircraft but couldn't make out much on the ground thirty thousand feet below other than the occasional lights of a passing city.

The jumpmaster passed the signal letting us know we were three minutes out. We checked each other's parachutes, switched from the paneled oxygen on the aircraft to our individual bottles, made any final adjustments to straps and goggles, and stood. When the one-minute call came, we began to shuffle toward the rear of the plane, seventy pounds of gear strapped between our legs, forty-pound parachute rigs on our backs, individual oxygen tanks on each man's side, and hoses running up to the Darth Vader–style O2 masks strapped to our faces. Rifles were lashed to our sides, night vision goggles protruding from our helmets like a small set of antlers.

We must have been quite a sight to the uninitiated aircrew. I could see the wide eyes of some of the younger crew members who couldn't believe we were about to dive out of this plane into a sea of blackness over the middle of nowhere with the temperature minus-fifty-five degrees Fahrenheit. What they couldn't see under the oxygen masks were our ear-to-ear grins. We gave the crew a quick wave and threw ourselves out of the plane and into the night abyss.

The bitter cold and 120-mile-per-hour wind blasted me immediately. I counted down four seconds, then reached up to pull the rip cord that would deploy my parachute. A light tug pulled me into a vertical position, the noise of air rushing by calming and familiar. I was floating.

I looked up to confirm a good opening and saw a fully functioning bunch of silk over my head. I immediately began to orient myself, finding the other jumpers to line up with as we organized into a stack.

I left the toggles (brakes) that controlled the angle of my parachute stowed, using my hips and body weight to steer. My arms remained folded across my chest when I wasn't checking the GPS monitor or toggling my radio. It was still so cold at this altitude that if my arms were above my heart for too long, they'd lose blood flow and functionality.

I arranged myself in the proper position in the stack, twenty feet above and twenty feet behind the guy in front of me. The team floated like this for some time. Under the typical square military parachute, you descend at about a thousand feet per minute, though that slows as the air thickens closer to the ground. If you've done everything correctly, you begin to feel more comfortable as you fall, the air warming by the minute as your altitude decreases. On this jump, from aircraft exit to touchdown, we'd be soaring through the air for at least twenty minutes, covering around fifteen miles.

There was a feeling of peace and amazement as I flew nearly silently through the dark night at heights normally reserved for people in the comfort of an airline cabin. Everything came through night vision in a surreal green filter. As I floated, I could make out the mountains below, the valleys, various specks of light in the distance. The rest of the stack of parachutes all lined up in a neat little staircase. I was keenly aware that there were people simply living their lives below: truck drivers on night routes, people sleeping comfortably in bed, completely unaware that a team of heavily armed SEALs was gliding overhead.

As I passed through some wispy cloud cover, I saw the mountaintops coming closer and knew that we would just barely clear some of the highest peaks. Our drop zone (DZ) was on the side of one of those mountains, eight thousand feet above sea level, where the thinness of the air presented the biggest challenge. At that altitude, my rate of descent was still pretty fast, and I had to take that into account if I didn't want to crash into the side of the mountain at over thirty miles per hour.

Upon approach, I released the rucksack between my legs so it was dangling on a short line underneath me. The DZ was a small, relatively flat space about the size of a baseball diamond. It didn't appear to have any major obstacles, just a couple of big boulders I would need to avoid.

I would have to time my flare (the moment when I started

pulling on the brakes to change the shape of the parachute in order to create lift) early enough so I didn't slam into the ground, but not so early that the parachute stalled and dropped me straight down. I scouted out a line to the left of the guy in front of me, just like I'd done a hundred times before, flared my parachute, and touched down with the softness of a feather.

Needless to say, this was not my first jump. I had been in the SEAL Teams for over a decade. I'd gone through enough training to reach a level of proficiency where I could conduct such a complicated jump—a nighttime HAHO with my troop while breathing supplemental oxygen, carrying a hundred pounds of gear, and landing on a mountainside DZ.

It took years to get there. I had been taught the same way we teach and train pretty much everything in the SEAL Teams: first you crawl, then you walk, then you run.

The first step had been a rudimentary indoctrination to the fundamentals of parachuting, with static-line instruction. This takes place at Airborne School right after BUD/S and is notoriously simple. My progression continued with free-fall instruction, beginning with classroom time to learn the basics of parachuting and skydiving. Then I moved to practical application, actually jumping from an aircraft in free fall. Those initial jumps were pretty basic: in the daytime with no extra equipment, accompanied by an instructor and a jumpmaster. They jumped with me, helping stabilize me in the air and ensuring I pulled my chute at the prescribed altitude. Through a two-way radio, they talked me through steering and landing, and then they provided feedback after the jump.

The crawl, walk, run sequence continued. I next conducted night jumps, but slick (with no equipment). Then day jumps with equipment, night jumps with equipment, day jumps with supplemental oxygen, continuing to add complexities as I went: carrying more equipment and from higher altitudes with oxygen, then adding more jumpers or maybe a dog. Before long, I was running.

This build-up philosophy can be applied across all domains. At its core, the goal is to get properly grounded in the fundamentals so you can continually improve at whatever it is you do. If the fundamentals are glossed over or not properly developed, it will hinder your potential for future expertise.

Think of it as building a house. You want to start with a strong foundation, a base that can't necessarily be seen with the naked eye and that supports all future building. And the higher you plan to build, the stronger and deeper that foundation needs to be. If you're building a one-story wooden home, an adequate foundation could be a basic cement outline. If you're building a skyscraper, that foundation had better be dug deep into the earth, reinforced with iron and steel. Thus, the farther you want to progress, the more important the foundation. You can only go as high as your foundation will support.

I started out as an engineering major in college. Obviously, a strong foundation in math is important in engineering. I'd always had a natural affinity for math and was pretty good at it. But I was overconfident. I skipped classes and taught myself a lot of the concepts. I took shortcuts. Freshman year it worked pretty well for me. Calculus 1 and 2 were a breeze; I pretty much figured them out on my own. Multivariate calculus was a little more challenging, though, and by the time I hit differential equations, I was struggling.

I had built a straw house. By coasting through the foundational calculus courses earlier, I had started jogging before mastering the necessary fundamentals. Everything I had built on top of that cracked foundation was now shaky. After I realized my error, it took an inordinate amount of time and effort to break down the straw house and essentially start over with the basics.

Now, if my education had stopped at Calculus 1, I probably could have gotten away with my original foundation. But an engineering degree equated to building a multifamily home, so my foundation needed a lot of work before I could meet that goal. The longer it takes to recognize that, the harder it will be to rebuild.

I coach my kids in soccer, baseball, basketball, and football, and we heavily emphasize the basics. Properly shooting a basketball requires the right foot placement, arm angle, hand position, and follow-through. Throwing a baseball or football requires similar fundamental mechanics, accepted basics that provide repeatable results. If these basics aren't taught early and inscribed in muscle memory, habits will develop that later limit progress. A natural athlete with a strong arm may get away with throwing a football with a long motion or not driving off the back foot, but that strategy will come back to bite them later. Tim Tebow had one of the most successful college careers in history but couldn't make it in the NFL because of his elongated throwing motion. It had worked spectacularly for him for his entire life, but at its core, it was flawed. By dropping his arm to his hip, defenses were given an extra split second to read his eyes and make a play on the ball. Back when he was crawling and walking, the dearth of a mechanically sound throwing motion was covered up by natural ability. It wasn't until he reached the NFL that his straw house was exposed, and he was out of the league within three years.

When most people think of crawl, walk, and run, they look at it as a slow and methodical endeavor. The perception is that crawling is gradual and takes a lot of time to master. Then comes the same arduous process for walking. Finally you can start jogging, but you're not moving with any real velocity until you're running full speed. But that's simply not the case, on several different levels.

Crawl, walk, run doesn't have to be slow and methodical, nor does it have to happen linearly, as exact steps in a row. Often the basics of something can be sufficiently learned almost immediately, allowing you to speed up enough to start walking right away.

Baseball players are constantly refining their swings, honing the basics of hitting they began learning in childhood, like balance, load, coil, stride, hand path, weight shift, head position, ball contact, and follow-through. No matter how skilled they get, hitters never stop fine-tuning those foundational skills. The fundamentals (crawling) weren't mastered immediately, but they were (and should be) taught immediately. While developing proficiency, hitters are still playing and learning, adding complexities like trying to pull the ball, hitting to the opposite field, and adjusting their swing path for different types of pitches. Running is achieved with increased swing speed, power, placement, and consistent contact. The tweaking of those fundamentals doesn't stop there. To continue improving, they go back and revisit the basics, breaking them down further and making small changes. Only then can they continue to grow as hitters.

It isn't necessary or even recommended to attempt to master each phase before moving on to the next, as long as you properly complete the foundational pieces. Think of it as the opposite of one step forward, two steps back: in this case it should be two steps forward, then one step back to revisit what you previously learned.

Nor is each step siloed or static; they blend and transition into one another, illustrating how important it is to constantly refine the basics even while progressing forward. You'll find that the fundamentals change with time and increased proficiencies. Maybe the industry has changed or the competition has improved. For hitters, pitchers get better. If you're learning a new language, as you become more fluent, you'll discover additional verbs to supplement the rudimentary ones you learned in a 100-level course.

To clarify, you don't simply graduate from one level, forget about it, and then proceed to the next. It isn't a stairway on which you reach the next floor in a continual motion upward with no thought as to where you have been. Though the foundation must be established early in the learning progression, that doesn't mean you don't continually return to the basics. No matter how advanced you get, you're always going to revisit your fundamentals and attempt to perfect them. The best hitter in baseball still works with a batting coach. He still practices his stride, keeping his hands through the strike zone, his eye on the ball. The same lessons he was taught in T-ball. The day he ceases working on the basics is the day he will no longer be the best hitter in baseball.

As you change and your skills change, so too do your fundamentals. The faster you run, the more you'll need to revisit crawling. Building a foundation is not zero sum, either built or not. Additional building requires tweaks and improvements to the foundation to keep it strong enough to support that growth. The basics are never really "mastered." They need constant work and rework, and that amount of work is dependent on how high you want to go. This is why I didn't get stung by my insufficient math foundation in college until I was well into the running phase of engineering. As my house got taller, my skills and expectations increased accordingly. And they required a stronger foundation.

In fact, the best time to revisit the fundamentals is when you find yourself plateauing in whatever it is you do. The more you master the basic building blocks, the higher you will be able to build. There will always be a new gimmick or trick that promises to get you ahead faster or beat the competition. Some new analytic method or promise of big data. However, most of the time, these are very advanced techniques that are inappropriate for all but the highest level of experts and usually are a distracting noise that is more hindrance than help. Ever hear of the KISS principle? "Keep It Simple, Stupid." Translation: mind the fundamentals in any given domain.

In March 2011, the most severe nuclear accident since Chernobyl rocked Japan as a direct result of leadership not covering the basics. The Fukushima disaster was found to have been completely preventable if TEPCO, the Tokyo Electric Power Company, had taken some basic safety, security, risk assessment, and mitigation efforts.

One of the very basics of nuclear power is the cooling system. Loss of coolant can lead to reactor core damage, nuclear meltdown, hydrogen explosions, graphite fires, and the release of radioactive material into the atmosphere and/or groundwater or seawater. Investigations found, and TEPCO later admitted, that the company had failed to take basic necessary measures to prevent the ultimate failure of the cooling system, resulting in an unprecedented disaster.

Japan is geographically located in an area known for earthquakes and resultant tsunamis. TEPCO ignored multiple studies that showed that the power plant was vulnerable to tsunamis. They discounted the earthquake risk and failed to take the basic mitigation steps that would have prevented the disaster. TEPCO, in a striking admission in October 2012, said they had been worried about lawsuits, public perception of nuclear power, protests, and costs of mitigation *before* the catastrophic meltdown. In the grand scheme of things, TEPCO forgot the basics and instead focused on peripheral noise. As a result, associated costs of the accident exceeded $100 billion, and the loss of life in terms of cancer will likely reach the thousands. This disaster could have been avoided if someone had simply focused on the basics.

Knowledge is cumulative, and how fast you move from stage to stage is dependent upon many variables. It's not the same for everyone. Each domain has a different learning curve and foundational requirement. You also have to consider individual capabilities, along with the quality of instruction and feedback. Let's take someone learning to hunt. They could potentially progress from crawling to running in a few hours. Maybe they grew up around guns and have a natural ability to attune themselves to nature. After a quick tutorial from an experienced hunter, they could be ready to bag their first buck. Someone else may be scared of guns, uncomfortable in the cold, and have an inability to sit still. Maybe they don't have an experienced hunter instructing them and providing feedback. For that person, it could be a while before they're ready to sit in a deer stand, if hunt at all.

It's always easier for someone who is already proficient in an activity to go back to the basics for refreshers. Which makes sense: the rich get richer. But it's an important distinction. When you are first learning something new, the basics are the furthest you've gotten. Once you are more experienced, those basics are old hat—but no less important. In many cases they're more so.

Tiger Woods regularly makes changes to his golf swing. There are many reasons he does so—age, back issues, course layout changes—but he's always tinkering. Each time he changes his swing, he and his coach start with the basics, breaking it down at the most elementary levels—backswing, hip rotation, grip, and so on—and then building it back up. Because he is one of the best golfers to ever live, his velocity through the fundamentals is a lot faster than a novice golfer's would be. The lesson learned here is that no matter how good you get at something, real improvement, even at the highest levels, always goes back to honing your principles. No matter your level of proficiency, you always need to be mindful of how you got there. And as you get better, it should be easier to refine the fundamentals.

Just as you're always revisiting your foundation, understand that you never stop building higher (unless you want to). There are always additional heights to reach if your foundation is solid. You can always get better and learn more. There will always be someone better. If you *are* at the top, rest assured somebody is going to pass you. That's how records are broken. Eliud Kipchoge ran a marathon in under two hours. Someone will do it faster. You have to be prepared to keep learning and strengthening that foundation if you want to keep up with the competition.

Not prioritizing a strong base is a common but deadly pitfall. Organizations and people, either intentionally or unintentionally, skip over the necessary basics and then wonder why their ultimate mission failed. Often the answer is simple: it's because they put all their energy immediately into running and didn't put enough into crawling first.

When focusing on the end goal, it's human nature to overlook the hard work needed to achieve the desired end state. People see where they want to be without considering what it takes to get there. Why do you think so many people quit BUD/S? It's not that they can't physically do it. Everyone there passed a physical training (PT) test proving they have the physical makeup. But many see the shiny gold Trident (a nickname for the insignia that Navy SEALs wear on their uniforms) at the end and conveniently forget about the years of pain and effort it takes to earn it. No one shows up in Coronado ready to HAHO or assault a terrorist compound. We all had to crawl first. We continually went back to the lessons learned during our time at BUD/S, whether it was to utilize a swim buddy, know the importance of maintaining our equipment, or refuse to quit. Those who weren't willing to put in the work to crawling never made it to running.

Businesses often talk about building leaders within their organization. They strive to be thought of as leadership breeding grounds for their employees, but often they don't put in the necessary infrastructure to allow that to happen. The people they purport to be grooming as leaders are never shown how to problem solve and make the tough decisions that leaders must make.

This is especially problematic in large bureaucracies. Due to a decrease in risk tolerance, major decisions come down from the top to be pushed out by middle management. The younger "leaders" issuing the directives are often not the ones making the decisions. By not being involved in that process, they might not fully understand the strategy behind the policies they are implementing, not to mention missing the opportunity to learn how those decisions are made. This hurts the organization in the short term—if a leader doesn't know why quotas are going up other than that the company wants to make more money, it's harder for them to manage the change—as well as the long term. When they are eventually promoted and put into positions to make those high-level executive decisions, they'll have no experience doing so, leading to poor choices. To compound the issue, they'll simply issue their directives to the next generation of middle management, who in turn won't have a foundational understanding of dynamic decision-making, and the cycle will continue.

If you're not grooming leaders to make decisions and allowing them mistakes, they aren't going to be able to think through bigger issues and make the right decisions. They need some autonomy if they're going to grow into true leaders, with a support infrastructure in place that includes mentors and formal feedback loops.

This doesn't mean just sending them to professional development classes or a workshop on leadership. While these controlled environments are useful to an extent, classroom instruction and learning need to have a practical component. Leaders need to be given the opportunity to practice decision-making in the wild if they're going to be able to do it when it counts.

It happens all the time in the military. Officers are thrust into leadership positions simply because of their tenure (resulting in rank) and their ability to play politics. We call it "yes man syndrome." Those prequalifications don't necessarily mean they have the background, experience, or ability to lead. I've certainly seen my share of incompetent leaders.

I had one commanding officer who was completely devoid of any leadership abilities whatsoever. Luckily, I realized it quickly and didn't incorporate his lessons into my leadership foundation. Instead of learning from him how to lead, I learned what not to do.

This guy immediately made it clear that he had a closed-door policy, which I had never heard of before. Other nuggets of wisdom he imparted to his junior officers, ensuring they would get no foundational leadership knowledge from him, were pieces of advice like, "It's not how good you are at your job, it's about making sure your superiors think it's easy to work with you," "Find a job where you aren't rated against your peers," and "Keep a low profile, don't take risks, and eventually you'll be promoted." I suppose it worked for him, because he made captain and spent thirty years ensuring his junior officers had a poor example of leadership to follow. His legacy followed him: some of those junior officers were promoted to more senior positions based on those flawed leadership philosophies and then imparted them to the next generation of officers.

Those without a baseline for leadership can lack the initiative and ability to make decisions. Instead they fall back on formal authority and start barking orders rather than being confident in their own decision-making and wielding the authority tacitly granted to them by their followers. They end up making poor decisions or no decisions at all (which they don't even realize is a decision in and of itself). This leads to degraded morale, a culture of frustration, not retaining good people, and promoting other poor leaders. In the military, it can result in lives lost.

Preventing this is a shared responsibility.

If you are at the top of the organization and you want the people who report to you to be empowered to make the right decisions and lead, you need to install a formal process of crawling, walking, and running. Start by investing in the development of the people in your organization. Create a system for professional development. It should include continuing education not designed for people to just go through the motions and check the box. Incorporate real-world practice that you, as a leader, make a priority. In addition to the classroom instruction, you should have a deliberate system in place that provides opportunities to not only make decisions but to observe the decision-making process at the next level. Start small and build. This can involve a mentoring system (remember the swim buddy idea?) or simply encouraging leaders to communicate the why and how of their decisions.

There isn't a one-size-fits-all model for every organization. Figure out what fits your culture and resources, and invest in your people. They are the foundation—the "crawl"—of your business. If you want to run fast as a unit, it starts with them.

As individuals, we are all responsible for our own growth. If we are not getting the support and foundation required to reach our potential, it's up to us to go find it. Books are an easy place to start. By reading this one, you've showed you want to elevate your critical thinking and build a strong leadership base. There are thousands more on any area of self-improvement you can imagine—some good, some bad; some that will apply to you, some that won't. Find those that do and read them. Implement those lessons.

Simultaneously, you can ask for more responsibility at work.

Tell your boss that you'd like to learn more about how policies and procedures are made. At the worst, you'll be looked upon as someone who wants to go above and beyond. Best case, you'll be included in some of the smaller decisions, allowing you to experience their process firsthand, giving you the opportunity to implement some of those tactics into your own decision-making. You'll also better understand the "why" of the things your organization is asking you to do. A win-win.

Start small—don't ask to own the nationwide profit and loss for the entire company. If you're in sales, ask for a stretch project in marketing. Find a mentor who will peel back some layers for you. As you progress as a leader, mentor someone else. You'll continue to advance as you educate yourself, adding more and more tools to your kit. But don't get lost in all the nuanced pieces you're adding as you walk and run; continue reading leadership books and case studies, always have a mentor or trusted sounding board, and continue asking questions to set and reset your foundation.

As you move through the steps, you'll start adding the traits of a good leader to your repertoire. More layers, more skills, more responsibility. You'll work yourself up the ladder until eventually you're running as a leader. When that happens, setting a base to foster leadership skills will then be incumbent upon you.

As previously discussed, progress through the steps is not done at the same pace by everyone. Even a skilled and experienced COO who comes to a new company would be well advised to crawl while learning a new culture, its bureaucracy, and the company politics. While that COO may be quickly running when it comes to implementing a new project management workflow, she will have to build relationships with her new coworkers at the most basic level until trust and rapport can be built and established.

Sometimes you'll be running on one level while crawling on another. We call these "connected verticals." Take mixed martial arts. A fighter may be a world-class boxer but an inferior grappler. He's running as it pertains to boxing but crawling on the mat. Recognizing this will allow him to place his energy and focus where it needs to be. This happens anytime we learn something new. Growth requires challenge. Don't make the mistake of thinking your expertise in one domain extends to another. Take the time to learn the basics of the new domain, even if you consider yourself an expert in a related field. You'll find a shorter learning curve, similar to how an experienced salesperson will have a shorter crawl than someone making a career change or fresh out of college. While both will have to learn a new product and sales process, because the experienced person has a strong base already, they can move through the basics quicker.

As a leader, it's important to understand the difference in progressions. You can't expect the person with no sales experience to close the same amount of business as the one already walking, just as we didn't expect a new guy who had never jumped before to be ready for a HAHO jump right away. But while we were empathetic to beginners, we also understood it was both parties' responsibility to move quickly and efficiently through the basics.

This book (and chapter) is about thinking differently and more deeply. Look beyond the literal and linear idea of crawl, walk, run. Ultimately, this is about putting a priority on the fundamentals and building a strong foundation. Then, as we progress, we ensure that we revisit, update, and maintain that foundation. At the same time, we live in a world of constrained resources and are often placed in situations where we feel as if we are not prepared or unreasonable demands are being placed on us. That's life; deal with it. If you find yourself overwhelmed or lost in business or in life, go back to the basics. Crawl, walk, run.

8

THE MORE YOU SWEAT IN TRAINING, THE LESS YOU BLEED IN WAR

We had just been tasked with a ▮▮▮▮▮▮▮▮▮▮▮▮ mission. The target was the usual bad guy, with intelligence suggesting he had arranged for passage out of the country on a small cargo ship. We had the description and location of the vessel; our job was to move into the area undetected, conduct reconnaissance, verify the target was on board, then board the ship and interdict the target.

The mission was a long and complicated one that would test the full complement of our skills as frogmen. The plan called for us, under the cover of darkness, to deploy on a river ▮▮▮▮▮

██

██

█████████████████████████████████████. Once we hit the water, we'd ██████████████████████ drive ████████ downriver to ████████████████████████ the   target. ██████████████████████████████

██████████████████████. Before daybreak, our reconnaissance teams would ███████████████████ get eyes on the target. Then we'd all stay concealed and wait for the target to arrive.

The jump into the river had gone off without a hitch. ██

██

██████████. It was ten o'clock at night. Once I heard the hydraulics start lowering the ramp, cool air rushed in. I watched the boats drop into the night, and my team quickly followed ████████ ████████████████████████████. Within seconds, I had the full bloom of my big round parachute overhead, and I began to steer into the wind to ensure I splashed down near the boats.

I was on a good course, so ████████████████████████ ████████████████████████████████. I went through the procedures for a water landing, ████████████████

██

██

██

██

██████. Though the current of the river was a challenge, ████ ██ ██████████████████████████████████████. We started down the river, eventually pulling the boats ashore at a heavily wooded area where we spent the remainder of the night concealing them and ourselves.

For the next ███████████ phase, we stayed hidden in the woods with round-the-clock surveillance on the ship. Intelligence indicated that if we observed preparations for the ship to get underway, we'd have ███████████ to react and board the ship to get our guy. If he showed at all.

We had set up ███████████ across a small bay from where the target ship was docked. ███████████

███████████

███████████

███████████.

Eventually, we got word on the radio that the crew was beginning to board the ship. We quickly slid into our dive gear and made our way to the water. At the edge of the bay, we all slid in, ███████████.

We were expecting a quick and easy dive. ███████████

███████████

███████████. However, it didn't turn out that way for me and my swim buddy. About fifteen minutes into the dive, the main compass he was using quit. No problem: two is one, one is none—I was carrying a spare. Unfortunately, I had no idea that his wasn't working. He had stopped swimming for a moment to mumble something to me through his mouthpiece, but I just mumbled back, "Whatever," not understanding there was a problem. ███████████

███████████. But since it's nearly impossible to communicate underwater when it's dark and you can't see two inches in front of your face, I never got the message. He thought I was using the spare compass to guide us, and I thought he was still driving. Basically, we were just swimming in random directions, and neither of us realized it.

██████████████████████, I could hear the pier, so I figured we were on the right track. The mussels and barnacles attached to piers give off a distinct crackling sound underwater, and that sound was getting louder. But after another five minutes, the crackling began to fade. What was going on? Did we just pass right through the pier? I hadn't seen any pilings. ██████████████ ████████████████████████████████. We hovered in the water about fifteen feet below the surface and tried communicating again. I asked in a gurgling underwater voice, "Where are you going?" He replied in the same muffled voice, "I don't know, you have the compass."

Crap. "I don't have the compass, you have the compass!" I exclaimed.

"Compass died twenty minutes ago!" he replied.

Great. We had been in the water for ██████████ already and were starting to push the timeline. I went to the spare compass on my wrist and we started on a new bearing, hoping to hear the pier soon and figure out where we were. After about ten minutes, we heard the familiar crackling sound and followed it all the way to the pilings.

We ditched our dive gear under the pilings, ██ ██ ██████████████. But it soon became clear that we were in the wrong spot, a good hundred meters away from the rendezvous point. I communicated via radio to my boss that we had surfaced and would be at the link-up point in about ten minutes. All he said was, "Roger, hurry up."

We had screwed up. I was dreading being the last dive pair to arrive and having everyone wait on us. We double-timed it and got there only to discover that we were the second dive pair ████████ to arrive. I couldn't believe it. The other pairs had had just as miserable a time. One pair had to emergency surface and swim back to the ████████████████████ because one of their dive rigs had failed. Another hit the pier even farther away than we had, and another went right through it and out the other side. Eventually, everyone corrected and made it to the link-up point. But the dive had taken three times longer than we had estimated, and we were all near hypothermic. Didn't matter, we had a job to do. With barely functioning, frozen hands, we ████████████████████████████████ made our way to find the target. ██ ██████████████████████████████████.

We ██████████████████████████████████████ ████ charged onto the bridge. I could see two guards as well as the primary target and immediately engaged the closest guard. I brought my sights up to eye level and squeezed off two rounds square in his chest, while my teammates did the same to the other one. I watched the rounds explode blue paint all over his chest and shifted my sights to the target, who quickly gave up. Mission accomplished.

This, of course, was only a training mission, albeit a difficult one. ██████████████████████████████████████ ██████████████████████████████████████ ████████████████████████████. There were no time-outs, no instruction along the way. Feedback came later. ████████████ ██████████████████████████████████████ ████████████. The blue paint was from the simulated munitions I had shot the "guard" with—nonlethal plastic bullets that still hurt like hell. ███

███

███

███. The idea was to make the training as realistic and challenging as possible so we were ready when it was the real thing.

One of the open secrets to the SEAL Teams' success is the inordinate amount of time and effort we put into quality training preparing for war. There's an incredible emphasis on deliberate practice of all things combat: parachuting, boating, swimming, patrolling, reconnaissance, diving, rappelling, ship-boarding, marksmanship, close-quarters combat—the list could fill this book. We did it over and over, day after day, year after year, with specific feedback loops. Thousands of hours doing and reviewing to prepare for real missions that may take anywhere from minutes to hours to days. No one said it would be easy.

While there is no exact ratio, suffice it to say that at least 90 percent of your time should be spent preparing, practicing, and reviewing for the real thing, whatever that real thing may be. But not all practice is created equal. Notice above that I referred to "quality training," "deliberate practice," and "specific feedback loops." Practice on its own isn't good enough.

The ten-thousand-hour rule made familiar by Malcolm Gladwell in *Outliers* doesn't guarantee a level of proficiency. The most overlooked aspect of that rule is a tiny but important distinction: that time must be spent in *quality* practice. The quality of that practice is infinitely more important than the amount of time spent doing it. Your practice must possess the characteristics above if the more you sweat in peace is going to result in less bleeding in war. Because if you do something the wrong way ten thousand times or for ten thousand hours, you've just gotten really good at doing something poorly.

I've easily taken ten thousand golf swings. And I could take ten thousand more, but my golf game isn't going to get significantly better. That's because I'm not incorporating the characteristics required of quality practice that will allow for significant improvement. If I really wanted to become a scratch golfer, I'd hire a swing coach. We'd videotape my swing, and together we'd break it down. We'd look at each piece—grip, hand placement, feet width, backswing, hip rotation—and make improvements. We'd analyze each aspect of my game—driving, long irons, chipping, putting—and put together a plan to get better. We'd set goals, develop actions to achieve them, and then we'd review our work. Only then would the training be optimized.

For me, that type of effort and investment isn't worth it, so I'll continue duffing my way through eighteen a couple weekends a month. It's another cost-benefit analysis we all have to make. It goes without saying that in order to improve, you have to put in the work. But it has to be the right work, and you have to be willing to get uncomfortable while doing it. If it's easy and fun, you'll never improve.

If your "practice" for a test is simply listening to your teacher lecture, you probably won't be happy with your grade. Without deliberate, designed study, you're just going through the motions and limiting advancement. Likewise, if a formal feedback loop isn't incorporated into the plan, the same thing will happen.

Any feedback should not be ad hoc; it needs to be regular and specific. "Regular" means that the one receiving the feedback has an expectation of when they are going to get it—once a quarter, after every game, at weekly meetings, whatever. It needs to be predictable. "Specific" means that it needs to encompass both the positive and negative, and go beyond the general "good job." If I'm getting feedback from a coach on my golf swing, the coach telling me "good swing" doesn't cut it. I need to hear that my hip turn was good, that my club path was too steep, that my feet were aligned with my shoulders.

Intentionally reviewing what you've practiced with a nonpartial third party is necessary to learning and improving. Someone who is going to see things that you, as an active participant, can't or won't. Could you imagine a football team without a coach? The feedback a coaching staff provides players is crucial for development and growth. It could be as simple as telling the quarterback to keep his eyes upfield, or as formalized as weekly film study and full evaluations at each position—who did what well, where there is room for improvement. Without those assessments and adjustments, how much better do you think the team would get?

Feedback loops are just as important in a work environment, but they usually aren't given the same priority as they are in sports. How many employees get regular and specific feedback from their boss? How many companies require recaps after a sales pitch or project completion? Not many, I'd argue. And often, when they do, they consist of off-the-cuff remarks based on limited firsthand knowledge and without follow-up. Or they're comprised of an annual review amounting to an hour-long check-in for the sole purpose of being able to say one was done. No real thought is put into the feedback nor to what is being reviewed. No actionable items are implemented from the review. Usually, it's more of a generic discussion about what the employee did well over the past year and reviewing sales numbers or metrics rather than a formal review of customer interactions or implementing policy. Those limited efforts don't help anyone get better.

Feedback is a form of reflection—both from the perspective of an individual and of the group. Feedback loops should consist of three parts: a) a review of the behavior or actions that occurred; b) the impact of those actions, both on you and your team or organization; and c) the future vector—what are you or the organization going to do moving forward? Notice that I didn't distinguish between positive or negative. Feedback should have equal parts positive and negative critiques. It's good practice to amplify the positive actions and tamp down the negative.

In the full mission profile above, the end result was the successful takedown of the bad guy. Mission success? Yes, at the meta level, but there were lessons to be learned that could improve our execution on the next exercise or real-world mission. After examining what we did well and what went wrong, we made changes to some of our operating procedures. Moving forward, we decided that we should arrange our gear differently. We refined the link-up and communications procedures. We learned that we'd have to consider metal in harbors that could mess with our compasses. Without having failed in practice, we wouldn't have been able to improve our techniques. And without the recap after the exercise, we wouldn't have identified those areas for improvement.

Our reviews were not just random exercises. We always had a leader guiding them. It may have been the platoon chief, the officer in charge, or whoever had the greatest view of the overall system, but that leader essentially became the moderator for the conversation.

Then we looked at the mission as a holistic system. How did it go overall? We broke it down into chronological parts and discussed each individual piece. Everyone added their perspective or perception if they thought it was significant or differed from the majority view.

The entire time we looked at the impact of each action not only on the individual pieces but on the system as a whole. Finally, we identified what we wanted to reinforce in the future, what deficiencies we were going to tackle, and how we planned to do so. Could be more practice diving in harbors, changing the standard operating procedures, or modifying tactics.

The reviews didn't take long, maybe an hour for a mission that lasted four days. Although we would continue to reflect on both the positive and negative long after the mission was over, we needed to execute a quick hotwash while everything was fresh in our heads.

Take the above training exercise. We started by evaluating each aspect of it. How did the jump go? Good. Rigging worked, parachutes opened, drop location was perfect. Any issues? Nope. The boat setup and derig? Good, smooth. The river transit? Overall, smooth. We should consider bringing a higher ratio of extra motors on river navigation. We encountered more debris than on ocean transits, and we were down to our last spare motor. The recon? Snipers were in place before daybreak, communications were good, rotations were sufficient to keep eyes on target 24/7. The dive? Ugh. Lots of improvement opportunities there. We didn't anticipate the metal at the bottom of the bay that messed up our compasses. There also were too many people linked together on a single dive line. Nearly everyone was flirting with hypothermia, so we decided to look at different wetsuits. The takedown went well, partially because previously we had trained extensively on that aspect and applied lessons learned in past iterations. We didn't look at our mistakes as failures; we looked at them as opportunities to get better.

Conducting a structured review loop and implementing those changes meant we'd be better operators and a better team in the long run. We'd take those lessons, apply them to the next deliberate practice iteration, and make further improvements. By the time these tactics would be used in a combat setting, we'd be familiar with different scenarios, have developed muscle memory to handle them, and be able to adjust to inevitable outside influences because we'd practiced it in training, reviewed the results, and made improvements.

The more deliberate iterations with structured feedback you can execute, the more improvement you will make. Muscle memory and exposure to a variety of situations are key components to training and practice. Muscle memory effectively transfers actions from the slow, conscious part of the brain to the subconscious, faster-responding portion. This can be both positive and negative. Without feedback, it can establish bad habits and ingrain them into our subconscious just as easily as the positive. Again, this is why feedback is so important. Every iteration, no matter the activity—shooting, throwing a ball, conducting a sales pitch—starts to furrow a path into your subconscious. Feedback helps to make sure you are furrowing a path that will bear fruit.

Exposure to a variety of scenarios has a similar effect. These experiences and iterations provide a library for your subconscious to access and compare to whatever situation you find yourself in. Having more mental models in your library helps you to confront complex and changing conditions faster and with better results. When confronted with a new and completely unfamiliar situation, humans have a tendency to suspend thought and revert to the primal instincts of fight or flight.

In the documentary *The Last Dance* about the Chicago Bulls championship team, Dennis Rodman, famous for his defense and rebounding ability (among lots of other things) talks about going through thousands of iterations of rebounding the ball. He would get each player to shoot hundreds of shots and notice which way the ball tended to bounce off the rim for each player. Some had side spin and would bounce left, some were always short, some bounced straight up, but each player's ball had a tendency to act in a certain way from a certain distance. Dennis Rodman developed a library in his head of how each of his teammates' balls would act, allowing him to put himself in a position where the ball was most likely to end up.

The results speak for themselves, as he will arguably go down as one of the greatest rebounders of all time. Although many other factors went into his rebounding prowess, the conscious effort to create a diverse library of shots in his mind certainly contributed greatly to it.

Quality training also means pushing limits. As I said before, it shouldn't be comfortable. If it is and is just a fun activity, no real progress is taking place. It wasn't fun to stay concealed, wet and cold, on a riverbank for three days, but it needed to be done in training if we were going to do it in war. If your goal (and all quality practice must include a goal) is to run a marathon, how much closer are you getting to that goal if you just walk two miles every day? You certainly can start with that level of activity, but if you're going to improve, you're going to have to push yourself. You'll have to increase the difficulty to see progress. Start with walking, build up to running a 5K, then ten miles. Each time you get comfortable with a distance, you have to make it harder. It's all about pushing through plateaus and expanding experiences.

That's why it's important to get exposed to as many situations as possible. We've talked about how it's a complex world with variables you cannot control. And that's OK, as long as you recognize that inevitability and prepare for it properly. Because we know that if you've experienced something similar in training, you'll be better able to react. The more variables you prepare for, the more fluid and innate that reaction will be.

That's why MBA students run simulated businesses. And lawyers review case law and conduct mock trials before going to court. Political candidates spend days preparing for debates. Warren Buffett researches every aspect of a company before he buys it. That deliberate prework leads to successful outcomes. But for some reason, many people don't conduct that level of due diligence. Whether it's buying a house or applying for a job, they may go through the motions, but their research doesn't possess the intrinsic qualities we're discussing in this chapter. Then, when the house has dry rot or they don't get a second interview, they blame outside influences rather than their lack of preparation. Sometimes it's a good idea to look at yourself. Did I do enough preparation? Was it quality preparation that challenged me and had a goal and specific feedback? If you haven't seen something before and aren't prepared for it to appear, it's going to be difficult to properly deal with it when it does.

The legendary—if not dubious—"invisible ships" phenomena that struck natives on so many shores is a great illustration of our cognitive blinders.

Supposedly, when Captain Cook reached the east coast of Australia in 1770 (and, it was reported, similarly when Columbus, Magellan, etc. reached other untouched lands), the indigenous people never noticed (or at least didn't pay attention to) the huge ships sailing in their harbors. They had never before seen such monstrous structures: hundred-foot boats outfitted with sails like clouds, their masts taller than the tallest tree in the forest, bows larger than any building they'd constructed. The theory is, since they didn't have a mental mode or experience to reference, they simply didn't see the ships.

Richard Feynman, a theoretical physicist and Nobel Prize winner, was known for, among other things, his ability to explain complex subjects in simple, accessible ways. His book *Surely You're Joking, Mr. Feynman!* talks extensively about the importance of multiple mental models across many silos of specialization.

This too applies to our lives. It goes like this: The more you experience and reflect on those experiences, the more you learn. The more you explore a variety of domains, the additional mental models you have at your disposal will provide a broader perspective for you to draw upon when encountering the unknown. Mental models are guides to how we interpret the world around us and therefore shape the decisions we make when interacting with that world. If we have only one mental model or single worldview, our ability to make rational decisions is limited without us even knowing it. This harks back to the famous saying "If you're a hammer, everything is a nail."

So how do we gain additional mental models and broaden the framework that guides our decisions and actions? Practice (with feedback and reflection) and repetition, of course. In terms of general learning, we have the Feynman technique. Here's how it works:

1. Choose a concept you want to learn about.
2. Pretend you are teaching it to a middle schooler.
3. Identify gaps in your explanation. Then research further to better understand your subject and fill in those gaps.
4. Review and simplify. Do it again.

Let's use starting a new business. Write down everything you know about starting a business. The explain your business, simply, to people with varying perspectives, experiences, and worldviews. Get their feedback and questions. Recognize that you won't have all the answers. That's a good thing. Go back, do more research, and fill in the gaps. Then do it again. Completing that exercise will flesh out what you don't know and guide you to find out.

9

IT PAYS TO BE A WINNER

It was a cool morning with a light mist in the air and a bit of a breeze. I knelt down in the grass with my team huddled around me. We didn't have much time, and I needed to get directions out and have them executed as smoothly and as fast as possible. I laid out the plan quickly but calmly, looking for recognition in each team member's eyes that they understood the plan. I found intensity and excitement reflecting back at me. These guys loved what they were doing, and I sent them back out into the fray without hesitation.

The next thing I heard was the familiar cadence being barked out: "Down!...Set!...Hike!" The football came flying back to my son as quarterback in the shotgun position. He faked the jet sweep to the receiver in motion and rolled out to his right with defenders in pursuit. He made it within a couple yards of the sideline, planted his feet, and put everything he had into the long throw down the field to a wide-open receiver. The ball landed perfectly into the waiting hands of his teammate, and he ran into the end zone to tie the score.

These little nine-year-old warriors had competed with everything they had and were rightly proud of that final touchdown. But it wouldn't be enough. They ultimately went on to lose the game and end their playoff run. I could see the disappointment in their eyes, especially as they looked at the other team celebrating their victory. After some words of encouragement and thanks, I handed out the trophies the league had given us for participation or whatever. Kids took them with varying degrees of enthusiasm, one eye always on the winners. A similar game would play out the following week with my daughter's flag football team. But they would go on to win the championship. My son's trophy sits somewhere in the back of his closet, while my daughter's is still on display on her shelf.

There is a segment of adult society attempting to shield kids from the pain of losing. Their well-intentioned but misguided coddling ends up sheltering those kids, teaching them incorrectly that everyone is a winner. Not only are they incorrect, but the kids see right through it. In today's age of giving everyone participation trophies, the kids still keep score. I find that they innately understand there is a hierarchy to everything they do, and it doesn't matter how often adults tell them everyone is a winner. Even if there isn't a scoreboard, they keep track of who's ahead. They know who wins. Kids seem to understand what some adults have forgotten: that if everyone is a winner, no one is a winner.

It's another maxim drilled into us from day one of training. The phrase "Pays to be a winner!" gets barked out by enthusiastic instructors constantly during BUD/S. They shout it before every evolution, whether it be a sand run, shooting exercise, or boat race, hammering home the importance of not only coming in first place every time but competing and improving all day, every day.

Everything is a competition at BUD/S, and that bleeds over if and when you make it to the Teams. It's made abundantly clear early in your career just how much it pays to be a winner. Or more accurately, that it pays to strive to be a winner and hurts to be a loser. Competition pushes everyone to constantly improve. If you can't keep up, if you aren't competing, you will get weeded out, passed over for promotion, or even kicked out. We wanted people who were trying to be winners, whose very soul hurt if they lost. People who were driven to be better by competition.

In BUD/S, those who weren't keeping up or were holding back were sent to "the goon squad." Essentially, the goon squad was an additional butt-kicking "motivational" session for the lower half or third of the class depending on the evolution, usually while the rest of the class was resting or preparing for the next evolution of the day. It sucked to be in the goon squad.

Too slow on the group run? Your team finished last in a race? You were headed to the goon squad for bear crawls up and down the sand berms, eight-count body builders (think burpees on steroids), sprints to the ocean to get wet and sandy, then sprints back over the berms again. It could last ten minutes or an hour. You never knew. What you did know was that it was going to suck.

The idea was to motivate you to push through the temporary discomfort felt during a run or evolution in order to avoid the certain pain that would come with the goon squad. I was only relegated to the goon squad one time. For whatever reason, I had fallen toward the back of the pack on a long soft-sand run. As I reached the finish line, an instructor was waiting, directing those of us at the rear toward another instructor at the water's edge. It was only nine a.m., and it was going to be a long day.

For the next half an hour, we were punished for our slow run time with what would make any CrossFit workout seem like a breeze. Everything hurt. My lungs and muscles burned. Chances of throwing up were pretty good. Sand combined with wet clothes chafed every part of my body. My mind went into survival mode, and I became a zombie, just putting one foot in front of the other until it was over. When it was, I and the rest of the goon squad rejoined the class and continued on with the day. That was the last time that I was ever in a goon squad.

During Hell Week, individuals or boat crews who won races might get to nod off for a few minutes while the other teams did another race. They might have been allowed to relax and stretch after a run or gotten extra time to prepare their gear or get cleaned up. While it was nice to be awarded some extra rest, it was even better to *not* have to sit in the surf zone freezing or run up and down the berms for the umpteenth time because you had missed a cutoff time by thirty seconds or lost a race by five feet. It became ingrained in each of us to reach deep down and give full effort on every evolution.

In BUD/S, in the Teams, and in life, it pays to be a winner.

It's an important life lesson that despite some adults' attempts, most kids learn at an early age: winning is better than losing.

Winning pays psychological dividends like the brain boosting serotonin levels, giving its owner feelings of accomplishment and dominance. There are tangible rewards like trophies and prize money that go with being the best. Respect, adoration, getting the most desirable partners: these all go hand in hand with winning. Humans recognize those rewards as positives, and they strive to attain them. Most people, once they get a taste of victory, want to experience it again the next time they compete. It's only natural to want to be recognized for your efforts. Winning becomes contagious. It boosts confidence. Winning begets winning.

In order to win, you have to compete. Competition is a good thing. It provides a metric to measure your performance against others of similar capacity or ability. It provides motivation to perform. It highlights strengths and exposes weaknesses. It provides substantive feedback on what you need to improve upon so next time you can compete to win.

But losing is not the antonym of winning. That's an important distinction to understand. Despite our appropriate focus on winning, absolute victory—meaning without loss—is never the goal. It's not realistic to achieve absolute victory in everything you do. No one has a perfect record. And that's a good thing. Improving, striving to win every time out, *that's* the goal. Losing is how we get better. Without loss, it's impossible to grow. You can't learn from your mistakes if, in theory, you aren't making any.

BUD/S gets its share of absolute studs trying to become SEALs. Olympic- and collegiate-level athletes, brilliant, accomplished guys, just the best of the best. Some are at the absolute top in their athletic or intellectual fields. The star high school athlete and college recruit. Often these are the first guys to quit. After a lifetime of nothing but sustained success and victory, they can't handle stark adversity when it finally hits. They've never lost before or experienced not being the best. And it's hard for them to handle.

Maybe a guy was the champion high school quarterback and

starting point guard, got all the girls, had straight As, was popular, could jump out of the gym and bench-press twice his body weight. That's all great, but there are plenty of guys like that at BUD/S. He's no longer special, and that's the first kick in the head for a guy like that. The instructors have seen plenty of these guys, and they want to know if he can excel when the going gets tough. He'll be singled out to see how he handles it. For example, the instructors will say, "OK, we're doing one hundred flutter kicks. If *everyone* can keep proper form and not let their feet touch the deck, you'll be secured and can go home." Then they'll single out that guy after eighty flutter kicks and say his feet hit the ground or he wasn't doing it right and make the whole class start over. Doesn't matter if he was doing the exercise right or not. Then they'll do it again. They'll watch to see how he responds. Does he take it stride? Try harder? Get frustrated?

The other great differentiator is the cold water, being immersed in the cold Pacific until you're on the edge of hypothermia. The cold is an amazing equalizer and truly tests your desire to become a SEAL. Natural athletic ability or being a CrossFit champ isn't going to help when you're freezing. Every muscle in your body is contracting, your lips are blue, your teeth are chattering from uncontrollable shivering. If you've fought and competed your entire life, experienced loss and adversity, gotten back up after getting knocked down, you can take the cold. If you don't have the inner drive to compete, to win, to overcome adversity, you will ring the bell and quit. The cold tests what you're mentally made of. The guys I know that made it through would never have voluntarily gotten out of the water because they were too cold. It's not an understatement to say that most would have died in that water before they admitted defeat and quit.

For people who have never felt the sting of losing, who have never had to search for the inner fortitude to dig deep and pick themselves up when things got really tough, it's easy to panic and crumble under the pressure. Like anything we haven't experienced before, it's hard to do when it counts. That ability to forge ahead when times are the bleakest is what it takes to make it through BUD/S. The SEAL Teams are about not just handling but excelling through adversity. The format and instructors ensure no one gets through without a hearty smack of adversity.

Winning is relative. It's not a zero sum game, with just the person, team, or organization that comes in first, wins the championship, or gets the deal the ultimate victor. Like all our maxims, this one has some dichotomies associated with it. And one of those dichotomies is that there isn't always just one, single winner. And just because you came in second—or last—doesn't mean you're a loser. Competition isn't limited to strictly external entities—you're also competing against yourself.

The BUD/S obstacle course is set up in the soft sand alongside the Pacific Ocean, designed to be completed in combat boots and long pants. When I first classed up, the standard, if I remember correctly, was twelve minutes to navigate these twenty or so obstacles. What they didn't tell us until the second time we ran the course was that we weren't only competing against the rest of the class but also against ourselves. Pays to be a winner. The instructors had our first time written down, and we had better be faster the second time through. If not, you could rest assured you would soon find yourself a "sugar cookie." This enjoyable motivational tool entailed sprinting down to the freezing Pacific Ocean, jumping in, then rolling around in the sand until you were covered in California's finest grit from head to toe. Then you sprinted back to rejoin the class and run the course again. Hopefully faster, if you didn't want to find yourself on the goon squad.

At the same time, we were competing against that week's standard. If the time to beat started at twelve minutes, maybe it was eleven by week two and 10:30 the following week. Of course, even if you beat your time from the previous week but still missed the overall standard, there was a corresponding punishment. That's why it was imperative to always be competing, always striving to win, even if you knew you weren't going to be the fastest in the class. There were still other metrics that defined winning and losing.

That's the lesson: you can't always be first, but you must *strive* to be first. Not everyone is at the same skill level, and that's OK. You don't need to compare yourself against the absolute best— if you played Rafael Nadal in tennis, would you be upset that you lost? You shouldn't be. You should still try to win, and you should still compete as hard as you can, but there is no realistic way you're going to beat him. Don't beat yourself up when you're competing outside of your level of proficiency. It's important to put your "loss" in context.

If you started a retail organization and the first year your gross sales were a million dollars, does that mean the company is a failure because Amazon did 142,000 times that? Of course not. That's not an apt comparison. But what if your profit margin was 10 percent? That's significantly better than Amazon's 4 percent. Did you beat Amazon? Wrong question. You weren't really competing against Amazon. What's important is that next fiscal year you increase your company's revenue and profit margin. That's winning. Competing against yourself. Remember, winning is relative.

There is no such thing as equality of results. The truth is, we aren't all created equally. I know that's a distinction from what's accurately written in the Declaration of Independence: we are all afforded the same rights, but that doesn't mean we aren't all different. Some people are just better at certain things. They're smarter, faster, stronger. That's a good thing. It's a measuring stick that we can all use to gauge and monitor improvement. Knowing this should make us all strive to be better.

The reality is, not everyone can become a SEAL. Nor can everyone be a doctor or lawyer or successful entrepreneur. Again, not a bad thing. In fact, it's destructive to say that everyone is equal and entitled to equal results. Do you want someone operating on you because society said that they can be a doctor when they weren't able to pass medical school? Results matter. If you graduate from the top of your law school class, you're probably going to get a better job and get paid more. Jimmy Garoppolo went 2–0 with the New England Patriots, then was traded to the San Francisco 49ers, where he started 5–0 and was signed to one of the most lucrative contracts in NFL history. Would he have received that contract if he played the exact same way but his teams went 0–7? I doubt it. In his case, it literally paid to be a winner.

It's just further evidence that there are definite and defined hierarchies based on your record. Elitism not only exists, it's needed. Life is a meritocracy, and we should want to lead and win. If a salesperson isn't competing and doing everything they can to win a deal, then what's the point of even showing up at work? No one is trying to be second place. However, if you don't get that deal, it's important you learn from it. Too many people blame outside factors for why they didn't win. They make excuses instead of looking within and figuring out what they can do better the next time. It's up to each of us to recognize those lessons; no one is going to do it for you. Society is full of people who don't get a job, who lose a deal, or who end a relationship and never take responsibility for it. Until you do that, it's going to be difficult to improve and win the next time.

On the flip side, if winning is too easy, you're probably not learning anything either. Competing in the proper domain is paramount to growth. As pointed out previously, if you play Rafael Nadal in tennis, there won't be many lessons to learn. If you play a child, likewise, your victory won't be very sweet.

When I play my kids in Ping-Pong, I win every single time. That gives me no sense of pride, it's just a fact. I don't gloat when I win, and they don't get too upset when they lose. That's the way the match is supposed to turn out. But sometimes a game will be close. They won't win, but if they make the game interesting, there's (rightfully) a small celebration. Remember, victory is relative. For them, coming close to beating their father is a win.

If you're a brand-new salesperson, you can't compare your numbers to someone who has been with the company for years. They have established clients, know the product inside and out, and no longer need regular training. You should be competing against yourself. Did you sell more in June than you did in May? Are you learning every day? That's the definition of success.

The goal is to be a better person every day. A better mother, father, employee, leader.

Don't ever play for second place, but when it happens, learn from it. Don't let it get you down, but also, don't accept it either. If you accept second place, your confidence will suffer, and you'll stop putting in the work to reach first.

One of my mentors in the SEAL Teams taught me that confidence is 90 percent of the game. Not fake, tough guy, "fake it till you make it" confidence—that type of overconfidence is easily exposed. He meant acknowledging and having faith in your skills and abilities and bringing them to bear with positive thinking. Other people will notice, and you'll enjoy more success. It's like the old saying: "If you think you can't do something, you're probably right."

10

WORK HARD,
PLAY HARD

This maxim is not exclusive to the SEAL Teams. In fact, it's a probably somewhat-overused saying today, a trite way of excusing partying or other reckless activities so long as you spend your eight hours a day at work. This is not what we mean by work hard, play hard in the SEAL Teams. The way we interpret it, and how it will be explained in this chapter, is not that common application. It isn't about how hard you play, or even how hard you work. Nor is it about the work/life balance cliché. It's not an equation: x hours at work equals y hours at leisure. It's about scaling your priorities and understanding the benefits of placing the same focus on your playtime as you do your worktime.

Our culture, rightfully so, dictates that hard work is a virtue. It's ingrained in our country's DNA, and it certainly plays a major part in why we're a world superpower. We teach our children the virtues of hard work from an early age. But that dedication to the grind can come at a cost if the play part is ignored or not optimized.

Americans place a heavy emphasis on our careers, and we often feel (I would argue incorrectly, but that is a discussion for another time) defined by what we do for a living. In many workplaces and industries, it's frowned upon to take time off, even earned vacation that is a part of our compensation. When I was in the Teams, no one wanted to be the first guy to go home for the day when we were stateside. Guys were reluctant to take leave, lest they be thought of as slackers. We fed off each other, leading to a culture of peer pressure that made guys work more than was often healthy. This strict emphasis on work, I believe, hurt our effectiveness in the long run. Guys needed to recharge their batteries to perform optimally. Both body and mind needed to heal, and people needed to spend time with their families. Often it didn't happen enough, and the work suffered.

People who are overworked make mistakes. And in our world, if someone made a mistake, it meant people died. If we were in a firefight or fast-roping from a helo or participating in any of the other dangerous activities SEALs undertake almost daily, it was necessary to be completely present and focused. We couldn't let our minds wander or attention slip; if we did, bad things could happen. Yet it was impossible to always stay at that required heightened attention level. Hence the need for downtime.

I had a boss in Afghanistan who epitomized this problem. He worked nonstop, putting in twenty-hour days and only sleeping for two or three hours. He'd get so tired by day three he'd make poor decisions, and then the fourth day he'd crash hard. He'd sleep for twelve to fourteen hours straight, meaning he was unavailable and leaving his men without a commander for half a day. If he had practiced balance and prioritized taking focused time away from work each day, unwinding, and getting the rest he needed, he'd have been a much more effective leader. There is no exact causation between his behavior and things that went wrong, but it certainly contributed to frustration and poor morale among the troops. This isn't good for any organization.

Every now and then I'd see the regular army soldiers in Afghanistan falling asleep during guard duty because they were run so ragged. They were doing yearlong deployments at a hectic pace, and it was impossible for them to sustain being on alert the entire time. Of course, if they were caught dozing, they were reprimanded and punished to varying degrees—often with additional guard duty. I believe that instead of punishing them for it, their leaders should have taken a hard look at what was occurring. Was the problem with one individual, or was the problem systemic? Could they have rotated shifts? Had a check-and-balance buddy system that rotated security at different intervals? I don't know the answer for each particular situation, but what I do know is that simply telling the guy to not fall asleep and then requiring he do more of the same wasn't getting results.

Likewise, in corporate America, a great deal of our identity is culled from our work. Especially in large corporations, it's a badge of honor to work extreme hours. When it comes to investment banking and some of the big consulting firms, you're not considered a workhorse unless you're sleeping at the office on occasion. In that industry, it's part of the business model: they hire the brightest, throw a lot of money at them, then work them as hard as they can until they burn out. Then they hire the next batch of MBAs and do it again. I would argue that model is outdated, and if those firms prioritized play—allowing their associates to recharge their batteries—they'd actually do better work in the long run. They'd have longer-tenured, more-experienced employees with clearer heads if they just allowed them to pace themselves.

This is not to say hard work isn't necessary and positive. It's to say downtime is equally necessary and positive. But more than that, you must put the same energy and focus into your off time as you do your work. Too often we're just going through the motions with our playtime, killing time until we go back to work. We're sitting in front of the television or checking email, not present in our leisure activities. That's an ineffective use of that downtime, contributing to burnout and less productivity at work.

Like the yin and the yang, there has to be a synergy between your work and your play. Without one, you cannot effectively have the other. Each contributes to the other. Just having play is not enough. You must be present, you must be focused, and you must put the same emphasis on that time as you do your work.

How often do we check our phones at the dinner table? At work, we have calendars and deadlines for our work. Why shouldn't we utilize those same tools for play? If you're simply sitting on the couch thinking about work, are you assigning the same importance to that time as you do to your time spent at work? Do you plan your downtime? Think about creating strategies and best practices to maximize it the best you can. I'm sure you do the same for work.

You can look at this time dedicated to yourself and family as an investment in your work. If you don't prioritize taking time off, you will see diminished results at work. If you're still answering calls or thinking about work during your off time, you're not truly recharging. Again, that will lead to burnout and ineffectiveness. Truly take that time and unplug. Do an activity that will allow you to forget that other half of your life, so when you return to it, you'll be fresh and energized. Hobbies and pursuits you are passionate about will energize you, and when it is time to go back to work, you'll have a renewed focus. So many of us think we're maximizing our downtime when we're really just going through the motions. When you are off work, be off work. Close the laptop; put the phone away. Be engaged and present, whether it's watching a game or having dinner with your family. If your mind is 50 percent on work and 50 percent on play, it's not focused on either.

As a boss and leader, it's your responsibility to make sure the people you lead are taking time away from the office. In today's world, that is no longer meant literally, especially as our society has further embraced remote work after the coronavirus pandemic. Basic technologies we all have access to mean work follows us outside of the office. Try email blackout times. Tell your employees to leave their laptops at work one or two nights a week. It's not only good for them, it's good for you. You'll have happier and harder-working employees. Turnover will be lower, productivity will be higher, and everyone will be more focused.

When I took over a platoon as a young lieutenant at SEAL Team Two, more than half the platoon members were legacy guys who had been in this platoon together for the two years prior. There were three or four brand-new guys, and the remainder of the platoon was made up of experienced guys coming from other platoons or other SEAL teams. It wouldn't be long before my chief and I discovered that these guys were burned out. They were just going through the motions, not taking initiative, waiting for decisions to be made, and had a general malaise about them. This was all easy to see even before we officially formed up into a platoon. We still had two years of hard training and a deployment ahead of us. No way were these guys going to be effective in their current state. Before we officially started our training schedule, we had an interim period of professional development where we sent guys to various schools for specific training and qualifications like jumpmaster, divemaster, breacher, or sniper. During that period we were also prepping gear, getting the training schedule organized, and assigning positions and responsibilities. After this period we would come back together as a unit and begin training as a full platoon.

Shortly before this occurred, we had a big party with all the guys and their wives or girlfriends. After the party got going, I was approached by several of the wives and girlfriends, at first individually, and then as a group. They wanted to know if they were going to see their husbands at all this platoon. I didn't understand what they were getting at. "Yeah, of course," I said, "why wouldn't you?" They began to explain to me that in the prior platoon, the men had worked late nights and every single weekend, at least Saturday and sometimes for a few hours on Sunday. I was dumbfounded, couldn't believe it.

You have to understand how our training schedules ran at this point in time. We would be on the road over 180 days a year at a minimum, usually in blocks of two to three weeks. Then, when were back at our home base, we still had local training, administrative requirements, and gear prep for the next training trip, exercise, or upcoming deployment. At the operational tempo that we ran at, guys burning out was a real thing. They needed playtime and needed to be present in that moment as much as they were present in the moment of work. If a guy's family life was not good or suffering, it would eventually bleed over into their work life and affect their performance.

I assured the wives that working a weekend or a late night when we were in town would be a rare occurrence, and I would do everything in my power to cut the guys away from work whenever I could. Our leadership group—me, the chief, and our leading petty officer—held true to our word. Nearly every Friday when we were at home base was a half day. We didn't work any weekends. Whenever we came back from a long trip, we tried to work in an extra day off that week. The effect on morale and performance was immediate. The guys were able to recharge their batteries and be present in their life outside of the walls of our compound.

You, as the boss, set the example. When your employees see you staying late every night, they innately feel like they should do the same. In the short term, that can be a positive thing. But working longer hours does not always mean more work gets done. It's a question of quality over quantity. As time goes on, everyone will get burned out. The work won't be the same quality. There won't be passion behind it. Take the long view and knock off early a couple times a week. Make sure your employees see that, and encourage them to do the same. They'll appreciate your management style that much more and come back the next day dedicated and recharged.

One thing we had going for us in the Teams was a love of our job. If you have that, if you truly enjoy your work, it's a lot easier to stay energized. It would happen all the time: we'd be ripping over the ocean in a Little Bird helicopter or rappelling down the face of a building, and someone would grin, look around, and say, "Can you believe we're getting paid to do this?" We loved what we did, and that helped us stay focused on the task at hand. But in some cases, it might have prevented guys from putting the effort into the playtime that is required to refocus on work. Because even when you enjoy going to work every day, you still need to get away from it to maximize effectiveness.

No matter what your job is or how much you enjoy it, there are going to be times you don't want to get out of bed. That too is OK. That's your body and brain telling you to take a break. That's an opportunity to prioritize play. Think about it: On those days when you have to drag yourself to work, how productive are you? If your workload allows it, take a day for yourself when that happens.

That's why we generally cut everyone away after a half day on Friday when we were home. Friday mornings we would have a physical training session like a long run (usually around eight to ten miles) or a monster mash. A monster mash was a physical and skills competition, usually done in squads or platoon-sized teams that took anywhere from a couple of hours up to three or four. A typical monster mash might consist of running a three-to-four-mile loop down to the beach and back with a fifty-pound rucksack, dropping the rucksack and picking up an inflatable boat, running with it to the bay and paddling out around a buoy a half mile out, then running with the boat down to the small-arms range. Here everyone would have to execute some course of fire with pistols or rifles and then run with the boat back to the compound. Scores and times would be tallied and a winner announced. After, guys would shower up, take care of some remainder work, and usually be out of there by noon. They'd get some time to themselves, then come back Monday morning ready to go.

Guys appreciated it, and I could tell it made them work even harder the following week. They'd spend the weekend doing whatever it was they were passionate about. For some, it was simply reconnecting with their families. Others would go fishing or camping. We had guys who played the piano, brewed beer, fabricated metal. Me, I enjoyed eighteen holes or maybe a few skydives to replenish the juices. You need diversity in your life. Let your mind wander. Think about something other than work. Then, when you go back to it, you'll be that much more present.

This balancing act has thus far been focused on not being as present during downtime as we generally are during work time. But there is certainly a segment that errs too far in the opposite direction, placing a disproportionate emphasis on play. Again, it's a push and pull. You can't have an appropriate dedication to one without the other. Just as if you focus too heavily on work, your productivity will suffer, neither can you only prioritize play and leisure.

I spent a lot of time in South America during college and afterward in the military, where the priority for the locals was, for the most part, play. I saw trainings canceled or delayed. Initiatives never got initiated. Nothing ever seemed to kick off on the timeline it was supposed to. If something could wait until tomorrow, it usually did. For us, it was the opposite: don't put off till tomorrow what you can get done today. The culture differences were a stark eye-opener, but they helped show me how to find a balance, a middle ground that is more productive and sustainable than living at the extremes.

A Colombian I was working with once encapsulated the difference in our cultures pretty well. He said, "Dave, the difference is we work to live. You live to work." He was right, and I've worked hard over my life dedicating time to *not* working hard. Be careful how you read that: I'm not saying I'm not working hard; that's not the case at all. What I'm saying is that I try to put the same amount of effort and presence into my playtime. Again, that could mean just consciously focusing on watching a ball game with my son or watching my daughter play guitar instead of sitting next to them and thinking about the consulting session I have in the morning. Later, after they go to bed, I can prepare myself mentally for the next day. In fact, the time spent present and aware with my kids will help that preparation later in the night. But in that moment, my time needs to be 100 percent focused on them and that game or song.

The reality is, a lot of the work and career pressures weighing us down are self-imposed. Usually, if we stop to think about it, we'll realize that the world isn't going to end if we don't take that phone call or shut the laptop down. In fact, it's pretty narcissistic to think it will. So pace yourself. If everything is the number one priority, nothing is the number one priority. There are going to be days where you'll have to work sixteen hours straight. Other days are for vacation and relaxation. Know the difference, and put your full energy into each when appropriate.

Hard work is important. So is downtime. "Work hard, play hard" highlights the importance of each and ensures you tackle that playtime with the same verve as you do work. The two are not adversarial or in conflict with each other. Rather, they are complimentary, with each benefiting the other. Keep that in mind the next time you feel guilty about taking time off or aren't fully present during your downtime.

11

PAIN IS WEAKNESS
LEAVING THE BODY

I am a disabled veteran, and it's not because I got shot or blown up. But the ailments I deal with today are plenty painful, a stark reminder of the job I did for twenty years. This is by no means a complaint or regret, just fact.

I have compressed and ruptured discs in my lower back. Slipped discs and degenerative disc disease in my upper back and neck. Tinnitus from too many explosions and gunfire near my head. Major feet issues that got so painful when I was deployed to Kosovo, simply standing nearly brought me to tears. I was taking 2,400 milligrams of Motrin a day, and when I finally went to see a doctor, he told me I'd have to stay off my feet for at least three months for the plantar fasciitis to get better. Sorry, Doc, but I'm kind of busy here. So he shot me up with cortisone on a regular basis until I completed the deployment. All of the guys I know have similar stories, many of them magnitudes worse. Rotations of max dosages of ibuprofen and naproxen were the norm. We just referred to Motrin as "vitamin M."

But the Motrin and cortisone were only masking the pain, making the issues worse by enabling me to be able to fight through it. Not that I regret this option was available, but if I had been able to listen to my body, stopped, and rested it, I would probably have been better off then and definitely today. But that wasn't the mind-set (or an option) in the Teams, certainly during my time. It had been instilled in us since day one of BUD/S—and pretty much every day after—that "pain was just weakness leaving the body." We should embrace it. And we needed to push through it, every single day, whether it was BUD/S, training, or combat. I now know that clichéd saying is neither true or helpful. In fact, it's one of the stupidest sayings we have.

At BUD/S, each morning at daybreak (or earlier), we'd line up on the grinder and wait for instruction. Inevitably, an instructor would come out ready to mete out the morning's punishing PT.

"Morning, gents," he'd say with a sadistic smile. "Let's do flutter kicks. How about a thousand of them?" And for the next hour, we'd lie on the hard concrete, legs moving up and down as our tailbones got rubbed raw, backs aching, hip flexors killing. "Remember, pain is just weakness leaving the body," they'd yell out every so often, extra motivation as the torture went on.

During that phase, yes, they needed to weed out those who couldn't handle the pain. But SEALs operate in a life-risking field, and their standards differ from the general public's. Even so, it's never healthy to consume as much pain as you can take. Sucking up discomfort and pushing through healthy stress, yes, but ignoring true pain is counterproductive and dangerous.

The mantra of "pain is just weakness leaving the body" was first attributed to legendary Marine Corps officer Chesty Puller and has been adopted by military units and fitness centers the world over. It's a nice sentiment, but again, taken at face value, it is harmful. Interpreted literally as an absolutist statement is not how I believe it was intended. It's meant to encourage you to push your limits, not ignore what your body is telling you. Pain is definitely *not* weakness leaving your body. It's your body's and mind's way of telling you, "Hey, something's wrong here. Stop what you're doing and get this checked out before something goes really wrong." If you ignore that message, you run the risk of doing real damage. But in many sectors, including the SEAL Teams, we're taught that it's a badge of honor to ignore those indicators and push through the pain. The truth is, you shouldn't. You should take notice and an inventory of what's wrong. Then come up with a plan to correct it.

If a pilot ignored a bunch of blinking lights and alarms going off in his plane, what do you think would happen? A crash, more than likely. Which is why if he gets warnings something is wrong with his aircraft, he's going to get it checked out. We should provide the same attention to our bodies (and minds).

This isn't to suggest you should stop doing something because it is difficult, stressful, or uncomfortable. It should not be used as a built-in excuse to give up or give in when something gets tough. Discomfort should not be confused with debilitating pain; there's a significant difference between the two. Discomfort is required for growth in every domain. Discomfort is positive. It's necessary if we are going to push our limits and get out of our comfort zone, whether it's weight training, school, or learning a new skill. Pain, on the other hand, makes us worse. Unproductive and subpeak. It's important—though not always easy to do—to define the difference between discomfort and pain. There's a fine line between being able to recognize unhealthy pain and whining. Physical and mental toughness are needed to do it.

Having self-awareness is a learned skill, something that must be practiced in order to become efficient. Finding the line where you're stressing your body and mind in order to get better at something is extremely important. You should practice looking at the world objectively. Spend a few moments every day in self-reflection. Seek out feedback from others. These exercises can help you see past your own cognitive blinders and understand when something crosses the threshold from acute stress to pain or chronic stress. It isn't easy, but when mastered, it is effective. An ability to differentiate between stressors will allow you to challenge yourself and grow while taking the appropriate measures when exposed to unhealthy pain.

Of course, everyone's threshold is different and varies by setting. I couldn't have stopped a patrol when I was a SEAL because my back hurt. In that environment, there's no choice but to power through. But if you power through back pain at an office job, you're not making yourself more productive. More than likely, your work will suffer. You won't be as focused. For me as a SEAL, the job trumped those risks. But even on patrol, if my back was killing me, I still could examine appropriate countermeasures. Was there anything I could do to alleviate the issue? How about something as simple as taking Motrin? Probably, but remember, this would only temporarily mask the problem. I needed to figure out how to address it, not cover it up. Maybe I should have focused on exercises to strengthen my back. Maybe my core strength needed shoring up. Maybe it was hip flexors or tight quads. Maybe it was overuse and I just needed rest. Whatever it was, I needed to heed the warning signs and try to diagnose and address the root causes, either on my own or with the help of experts. An internal inventory was required. Nearly anything was better than saying, "That's OK, it's just weakness leaving my body."

There was a recent commercial where people talked about taking sick days, only to reveal at the end of the commercial that they were talking to their young children instead of their bosses. All parents know there is no such thing as a sick day when you have kids. You can try to take it easy and have your spouse pick up more of the workload, but there's no way to completely log off.

That's not the case at work. Yet often in today's culture, taking sick days is seen as weak or lazy. I'd argue that *not* taking sick days (when truly ill, of course) can be worse for the company than showing up. We all know that we don't perform at our peak when we don't feel well. How much good work actually gets done? And of course you run the risk of infecting coworkers. But we all know people who come to work no matter how sick they are, and we also know people who call off regularly. They have different thresholds and priorities.

In fact, those thresholds and priorities have already started to shift. With society ultraconscious of anyone with an illness and what it could represent, coworkers will undoubtably start casting long looks at their associates if they come into the office coughing or sneezing. A deadly virus and pandemic will do that—the cost/reward analysis has changed since coronavirus entered our lexicon. The line has moved, probably rightfully so.

That line does vary depending on context and personality.

The military trains for war. A chaotic environment where there are no time-outs for pain. The battle does not stop if you are sick or wounded. You have to be able to push through and still function no matter how many warning lights are going off. That's the reason for the emphasis on pain tolerance in the Teams: it's necessary for combat. In the real world, very rarely are the stakes as high.

For someone with an office job, it could be as simple as the example of sitting at a desk all day with back pain. Do you ignore the problem being communicated by pain and mask it with medicine? Or do you listen to what your body is telling you and try to fix the issue? If so, how do you go about fixing it?

You could get a stand-up desk. Maybe you need to join a gym and strengthen your core. Change your diet. Yoga or daily stretching can help. Rather than push through the pain or mask it, heed what it's telling you. Because that back pain is not weakness leaving your body. It's your body tapping you, saying, "Hey, we need to change something up here. If we continue down this path, we're going to really be in trouble."

We all have stresses in our life. Our toddler that won't sleep at night, therefore we can't sleep at night. A paper due at school. End-of-month reports at work. Carpools and bills to pay. It's easy to get tired, ill, and overworked. Those are natural parts of life, things that cannot be avoided. We have to be able to work through those normal stresses. That's the other side of the line between discomfort and pain. The acute stresses, discrete moments that are actually good for us.

But sometimes those stresses cross the line. They move over to chronic stress. After powering through for so long, maybe you're missing deadlines or showing up late to meetings. Maybe you aren't present at home, and your marriage is suffering because of it. Maybe you've been drinking too much, not sleeping enough, getting sick more often. At some point you have to listen to your mind and body. They're telling you that you need a break. And it's OK to take one. Take a mental health day. Sleep in. Let yourself recover. In the long run, you'll be more productive for it. If you're doing many things poorly, you're doing nothing well. Sometimes we all need to reprioritize for the greater good.

Everyone's tolerance is different, and everyone's perception of pain and stress is different. One person's pain is another's proper amount of productive stress. Pain encompasses a wide spectrum. It's important to know your limits and to push them, just not too much. The key is in the dosage. Acute stress in small doses produces cortisol in the body, and those small doses are good for us. Cortisol is called the stress hormone because it helps control mood, motivation, and fear. But if you pass into the realm of chronic stress or chronic pain and the dosage of cortisol runs unconstrained, it goes from beneficial to toxic.

Again, don't use this as an excuse to go easy on yourself. There's a difference between being lazy and recognizing that you're pushing yourself too hard. For example, doing burpees might not be comfortable. It may hurt a little. Your muscles will get sore and fatigued, but that's good stress. That's growth. For some, that number may be five burpees; for others it's five hundred. We are all individuals with different tolerances and experience. But regardless of your level of fitness, if you feel something pop in the middle of a rep, that's pain. You've pushed too far past your limit and need to stop and self-assess.

Most of our training in the SEAL Teams was designed in blocks. Depending on the type of training, blocks were anywhere from one to four weeks in general. The blocks cover things like air operations, land warfare, urban combat, and diving (otherwise known as combat swimming). One time we were doing a combat swimmer (diving) trip in the Newport, Rhode Island, area. This particular block was a little over three weeks long. For some reason, the training cadre was convinced that dive-training blocks had gotten too easy and that it was making us soft and weak. As a remedy, they decided the training should involve an exceptionally high amount of "finning" yardage. Finning refers to the act of propelling yourself and your dive gear through the water wearing dive fins. This isn't just like swimming with fins on; you propel extra gear and weight through the water at a consistent pace. On average, we were finning around six hours a day. This wasn't all underwater. Some of it was what we call turtlebacking: lying on our backs on the surface of the water when far from the target and transiting on the surface. We were allowed no ramp-up or adjustment period; it was high mileage from day one. I'd equate it to training to do a marathon by running a marathon every day. A week of this began to take a toll on everyone. I had several guys who had to stop training from eardrum ruptures, sinus issues, and tendonitis. By the end of week two, less than half the platoon was still diving. The training cadre was furious. As the platoon leader, I told the cadre it was too much and that they were hurting guys. Many of them were sympathetic, but the head of training was old-school. Pain was weakness leaving the body. In his eyes, we were weak and needed to harden up. I was furious. The tops of my feet hurt so badly I could hardly walk. I was limping everywhere, and simply putting my fins on made me almost throw up from the pain. But I didn't care. I was the platoon leader and wanted to prove to the instructors and my guys that I could take the pain. I finished every dive that last week, constantly downing Motrin during work and alcohol after to dull the pain.

This didn't make me stronger. It made me weaker for years. I had stress fractures on the tops of both my feet and severe Achilles tendonitis, both of which still haunt me to this day. It's not that the alarm bells weren't going off; it's that I ignored them for whatever reason—pride, the stigma of "being weak," wanting to prove myself. It didn't matter. I was stupid. This was training, not war. There is a difference. The lesson here is, don't be stupid. Listen to the warning signs.

When I was in the SEAL Teams, there was a real stigma about going to medical or getting things checked out. It was looked at as being weak, so we rarely got things checked out, and that was to the detriment of our bodies. Looking back, it was a mistake. Of course, in retrospect, nobody knows how things might have been different, but I suspect we did more harm than good with that philosophy. Guys with invaluable experience could have remained operational longer. I've heard that this mind-set has changed, and there is more of an emphasis on heeding the warning signs and implementing recovery and rest. Instead of encouraging guys to just push through the pain, it's now treated, and guys are having longer careers and are able to do more since their bodies are not breaking down as much. I also suspect and appreciate that after they leave the navy, their quality of life will be better. This isn't to say today's SEALs aren't pushing the limits of the human body about as far as they can go; they certainly are, but they're doing it in a more thoughtful manner. The training is informed by objective science, not subjective feelings and old-school mentalities.

You can see this adaptation with sports teams as well, from high school on up to college and through the pros (at least the good programs). They have incorporated nutritionists and physical therapists along with placing an emphasis on recognizing concussions and limiting contact in practice. Protective equipment is better now, and football teams no longer practice in pads in the summer heat twice a day while denying players water. Somewhere along the way coaches realized being dehydrated doesn't make you stronger. In fact, it does the opposite. At a minimum, lack of hydration decreases performance. At worst, it puts lives in jeopardy. Denying kids water doesn't toughen them up; it puts their health at risk, makes them weaker, and kills their ability to execute. It's evolution. Rather than being looked at as being weak, hydrating players is now looked at as an intelligent tactic for achieving peak performance.

This goes past the physical realm. Mental issues, depression, and anxiety are not weaknesses. They are alerts from your brain telling you something is wrong. If you ignore them, they aren't going to go away. Stigmas around mental health issues have been a little slower to wane, but it is getting better.

In the military in general and special operations in particular, historically there has been a stigma attached to acknowledging PTSD or other mental disorders. Shame was attached to injuries you couldn't see. In fact, until recent wars, we didn't even consider TBIs, or traumatic brain injuries, actual injuries. Now a lot of research is being done around these invisible injuries. The work is allowing us to stop seeing TBI as a mental disorder with questionable causality and start seeing it as a cognitive problem stemming from physical concussive forces and impacts. Hopefully the stigma is being lifted to the extent that we can recognize the problem's root causes and work on prevention and treatment.

The hushed atmosphere around mental issues is not unique to the military. People the world over suffer from depression, anxiety, and a variety of other mental issues in silence, either because they think they should push through the anguish or because they're too embarrassed to admit to someone else there is a problem. There could be an external factor causing mental pain—a bully, loss of a loved one, being fired—or an internal one, like a chemical imbalance or genetics. Either way, there is no advantage to "toughing it out." There is no shame in admitting you are having issues and getting help for them. I would argue that shows more strength than keeping it bottled in. We are all in this life together, and it's up to each of us to show compassion and empathy. Like in the burpees example, we all have different thresholds for different things.

Mental problems aren't always as easily recognized. There's no bone sticking out or shoulder out of its socket. But that doesn't mean the pain isn't just as real. And similar to physical pain, it can be difficult to discern between discomfort, and stress and pain.

One benchmark is to consider how much the issue is affecting your daily life and personality. Discomfort or stress, on a relative scale, is noticeable, but it won't affect your ability to go about your normal routine. As you move up the pain scale, you can become consumed by the pain. It impacts your life every day. You notice a decline in cognitive abilities as well as personality. This level of mental anguish needs to addressed.

Ultimately, when diagnosing and correcting both physical and mental pain, a nuanced approach is the prescription. The absolutist statement "Pain is weakness leaving the body" may sound tough, but it's the exact opposite. Use your head, think differently and more deeply, and grow different and better.

12

MIND OVER MATTER
(IF YOU DON'T MIND,
IT DOESN'T MATTER)

When I retired from the military in 2013, a couple of special operations guys I served with recruited me to come work at a big data analytics company out of Washington, DC. I knew these guys well and trusted them, and they had great things to say about the company. The pay was good, it was doing something I thought I would like to do, and the company had serious growth potential. "Great," I said, "I'm in." The plan was to take the company from a $15-million-a-year company to a $50-million-a-year company within three to five years.

I moved my family to DC and started running projects for them. It was going well for a while. But soon it became clear the CEO and the president (not the guys I knew from the military) were morally and ethically bankrupt. Serial liars who were set in their ways and unable to listen to anyone else's advice. The company started spiraling downhill, and within a year they had closed their doors and laid off 90 percent of the company with little notice.

Needless to say, that first professional experience as a civilian did not go as planned. I had grand designs on helping build the company and then all of us cashing out. Those expectations had been unceremoniously dashed. I was stuck in DC, suddenly unemployed, and not sure what to do next. I had a choice to make. I could let the failure affect me negatively, or I could learn from it and use it to my advantage.

Instead of complaining and allowing the failed job to bring me down, I chose to move forward. I chose to not let it bother me. I couldn't bury my head in the sand and ignore what had happened, but I also couldn't let it drag me down. There were aspects that would affect me no matter my mind-set—the loss of a paycheck, for one. But how it affected my attitude was completely up to me.

The company failing hadn't been in my control; how I responded was. Instead of adopting a "woe is me" mentality, I didn't let it adversely affect me. I put it behind me, chalked it up to a learning opportunity, and moved on.

It was mind over matter—if I didn't let what happened bother me, it wouldn't. I chose to use the experience to start a successful consulting company with one of the guys who had recruited me. We'd both learned a lot of good things from the failed venture, and we used them to our advantage in building the new company. It wasn't only that we turned misfortune into fortune; it was that we had decided to turn misfortune into fortune. It wasn't about what had happened; it was about our response to it. It was about making a choice.

People always ask me how I stayed calm on helicopters when we were being shot at or riding in a Humvee when we knew IEDs were out there. Easy. My answer: I made a decision to not dwell on it. There was nothing I could do about it, so I kept my focus on the important things that I could control: my job. What I'm going to do when we're on target. And so on.

It's the same mentality in the civilian world. Focus on the things truly within your sphere of influence. The people, places, events, and things that you can have an impact on. The only thing you truly control is yourself. Your responses, actions, words. The majority of your attention should be focused on those things you can control and their impact within your sphere of influence. Beyond that, you have to roll with the punches. Be alert and on the lookout for those punches. Try not to take them directly on the chin. If and when you do, get up and do it again.

I couldn't control whether or not a rocket or bullet hit the aircraft I was in. So I didn't worry about it happening. I did make sure that I knew where the exits were, where first aid equipment was, and that I was strapped in. Those were the things I could control.

Bad things that are out of your control are going to happen. If you allow them to drag you down when they do and to act like a victim, you will become one. It's a self-fulfilling prophecy. I tell my kids I don't want to hear them say the words "I can't." As soon as those words enter your mind, or worse, come out of your mouth, chances of success plummet. If you believe you can do something, you have a better chance of actually doing it. In many cases, it comes down to confidence.

A senior chief I worked with in the Teams whom I greatly respected instilled in me the value of confidence. I remember once we were conducting a full-scale training exercise in North Carolina. It was a short-notice exercise, so when we got recalled, I had to immediately rush in to start planning the operation. My immediate job as a troop commander was to collect the mission details, come up with a plan, and communicate it to my team so they could start prepping gear.

Essentially, the intelligence was that we had a group of terrorists in a small town, and we needed to go in and take them out. The plan called for us to free-fall from C-130s in the middle of the night, land a mile or two outside the village, patrol in to take them by surprise, then get out of there. A pretty standard direct-action mission.

Since I was conducting the planning and we were on such a tight time line, my guys grabbed my gear out of my cage for me. I had two bags set up for this type of operation ready to go, each with very similar equipment. The main difference between the two bags was the type of helmet inside and how the oxygen mask fit on each.

As soon as we finished planning, everyone rushed out to the planes. We did a final equipment check, going over weapons, putting on chutes, and checking the rest of our kit. That's when I put my helmet on and realized it had the wrong fitting for the oxygen masks. As configured, when I tightened it down, it pulled the mask up all the way up my face, basically over my eyes. Crap.

We always carried a jump bag with spare equipment in it (two is one, one is none), so I went to this senior chief to see if he had another mask that would fit my helmet. He quickly checked, but no dice.

"Dammit," I said. "This sucks. The O2 mask doesn't fit my helmet."

"That does suck," he replied. "What are you going to do about it? Are you staying back? Are you a no-go for this mission?"

"No, no, I'm good," I said. "I'll make it work."

"Good. Remember, man, this game is 90 percent mental. If you don't worry about it, it won't bother you."

"Roger that, Senior," I said, and boarded the plane.

What he was telling me, essentially, was to not sweat the small stuff. That if I spent energy and brain power worrying about the mask, I'd get inside my head and spiral downward. If I wanted to have a successful jump, I had to put the small stuff out of my mind and focus on the mission.

Now, some people might say that not having oxygen at twenty thousand feet wasn't "small stuff." But the senior chief was right—it wasn't a problem if I didn't allow it to be. If I was confident I could make it work, I could. Overcoming this obstacle was mental. I wouldn't allow myself to get hung up on it or let a seed of doubt creep into my psyche. In fact, I forgot all about the mask until we started our prebreathing procedures and hooked up to the oxygen tanks in the aircraft. Then, instead of worrying about the issue, I spent my energy figuring out how to overcome it. What could I do to make this work?

I started monkeying around with the mask. I tightened it as much as possible, then cinched it down and jutted my jaw out to kind of keep it in place. I could clamp it down enough that it was holding in the aircraft, uncomfortable as hell, but in place. I tried different strategies instead of worrying what could happen if I didn't have oxygen. I didn't get fixated on it not working. If I had, I would have lost confidence. I would have been thinking about what could go wrong rather than what could go right. And disaster could have ensued.

I felt good about it before jumping, but as soon as I left the plane, the initial wind blast immediately knocked the mask out of place. I now had an oxygen mask that was getting plenty of air to my forehead and eyes and goggles that were wedged under my helmet. Unfortunately, that's not how they were designed to work. "Uh-oh," I thought, "this isn't good. I'm not getting oxygen, and I can barely see while squinting into 120-mile-per-hour wind smacking me in the face."

But panicking would be the worst thing I could do. My focus went to finding a solution, to taking control of the things I could: my responses and emotions. I used both hands and grabbed the mask, pulling it back over my face. It allowed me to get oxygen, but now my hands were occupied. OK, as long as I could stay stable in the air, I would be good to go. I compensated by pulling my heels up to my butt to make everything symmetrical so I would fall flat and stable. I continued squinting tightly, tears streaming down my face from the wind, moving on to solving the next problem: seeing. With one hand, I held the mask over my face so I would keep getting oxygen. With the other, I positioned my goggles back in place so I could sort of see again. It wasn't ideal, but it was working. When I had to check my altimeter, I would let go with one hand, sticking the opposite leg out to compensate before going back to holding the mask in place again. If I let go with both hands, it would block my eyes. That wasn't going to work. Falling at 120 miles per hour, covering a thousand feet every six seconds, with another thirty or so jumpers in the air around me, meant being able to see was high on my list of priorities. Every now and then, I'd stick my arm back out and check my altimeter, counting down until I needed to pull my chute while holding the mask over my face with the other hand. When I reached pull altitude, I left one hand on the mask and used the other to reach up to my shoulder and pull the main rip cord that released my parachute. I was rewarded nearly immediately with the wonderful sight of a full canopy of silk overhead. I released my O2 mask, breathed a quick sigh of relief, and put the last ninety seconds behind me. On to the next challenge.

The mask issue forced me to change the way I positioned my body in the air. It affected the way I fell. It was uncomfortable. It sucked. It certainly wasn't the optimal way to be falling through the sky in the middle of the night. But I didn't make a big deal of it in my head. I stayed confident and completed the mission without anyone else even knowing I had a problem.

That wouldn't be the last problem on this jump. The spot for the release (the point at which we exited the aircraft) was off by quite a bit. By the time we were all stacked up under good canopies, it was pretty apparent that we weren't making the planned drop zone, a nice clearing on the edge of a forest. Instead we would be landing smack in the middle of the woods. Never fun. Once again, it was on to controlling what I could. Instead of focusing on how bad it was going to suck landing in the trees, I focused on what I could do about it. I thought to myself, "No problem, I got this." I looked for what appeared to be the softest-looking and least dense area of trees, steered my canopy toward it, and prepped for a tree landing. Arms protecting face, legs together, half brakes to slow forward velocity. I went barreling into the trees with full confidence that everything would be fine. I flew right between two large trees and was just about to land in a big bush when my chute got caught up on branches overhead. I was jerked to a stop, dangling about ten feet above the ground. As I began to begin working on this next problem, the branches holding on to my chute gave way, and I fell into the bush ten feet below. Problem solved. I gingerly started moving my body. Nothing broken, no holes in me—everything appeared to be in working order. I gathered up my gear, put that jump behind me, and got on with the mission, confident I could deal with anything that came my way.

Like that senior chief had told me, confidence is a prerequisite for success. However, there is a fine line between confidence and arrogance. Arrogance can doom you, while true confidence helps you succeed immediately while also setting a foundation for future success. The key is differentiating between the two.

How can you tell the difference between confidence and arrogance? It's not always easy, but here's my definition: A confident person has the ability to recognize the potential for improvement and takes advice. An arrogant person cannot admit mistakes and is no longer learning. Having confidence means you're able to recognize your mistakes. Then, instead of letting them cripple you, you decide to turn them into learning experiences. You can take advice and make changes so the same mistakes don't happen again. When you're arrogant, you think you know it all and ignore your mistakes. Thinking you're perfect is a dangerous sentiment.

Being confident allows you to listen to and embrace outside influences. Those perspectives are incredibly important to see things objectively. That's why leadership coaches and consultants can be such invaluable resources. Even if you aren't in a position to hire someone to help you see scenarios from a third-person viewpoint, I still recommend integrating a trusted, impartial observer. A friend, family member, or anyone unaffected by the situation can help you see the forest for the trees. They'll point out things you might not have considered being stuck in the hamster wheel of your own head. That willingness to be critiqued is a sign of confidence.

When you start to lose confidence, it can make you hesitate and lose focus on the mission at hand. That's when unnecessary mistakes happen. The confidence/mistake loop can be a vicious cycle, almost a chicken-and-egg situation: losing confidence creates mistakes, while making mistakes leads to a degradation in confidence. That's why it's important to have a short memory. When something bad happens, file it away, and don't let it bother you. It's important to learn from it but not to get hung up on it.

Let's say you get divorced. That's a traumatic experience for anyone. But does it mean you should never enter into another relationship again? Are you going to let that disappointment bother you so much that you don't try to find love again? Of course not. When things don't go your way, no matter what you do, they are going to bother you at some level. The key is not letting it cripple you to the point of inaction or making additional mistakes.

There are plenty of stories about successful entrepreneurs who had an impressive track record of failures before their companies finally took off. People who didn't let their setbacks set them back. Heck, Steve Jobs got fired from his own company. Fred Smith, who founded FedEx, was down to his last $5,000 and the company was in danger of folding when he took a trip to Las Vegas. Smith ended up turning that five grand into enough money to keep the company afloat for another week. During that week, he secured a new investor, and the rest is history.

Of course, I'm not suggesting gambling as a way to finance your company. But it is an example of finding a creative solution to a problem rather than giving up. Essentially, that's what you're doing when you let setbacks bother you. You're giving up. It's a decision that's all in your head. Mind over matter. "If you don't mind, it doesn't matter" refers to the mental aspect, not the caring aspect. It doesn't mean you should be apathetic and ignore lessons from past experiences or embrace some fatalist attitude that everything is out of your control. You are in control of how you respond to external influences. You are responsible for how you think, how you act, and what you say, regardless of the situation.

Getting stuck in a mental vortex after a setback can have to do with a perceived loss of control. But in truth, it should be the opposite. At no time are you more empowered than after a loss. What happens next is completely up to you. Do you accept that part of that loss was out of your control, then make a conscious decision to find the learning opportunity? Do you make a conscious decision to address the shortfalls that were in your control? It's true that sometimes you can't control the results that come from your actions, but that doesn't mean it's acceptable to leave it to pure chance. I firmly believe you can increase your odds of future success by taking control of what and how you think, do, and say.

A lot of young people in their teens to early twenties seem to get stuck in this spiral. They've grown up imagining how their life is going to look, and when they hit a speed bump, they fall to pieces and knock themselves completely off track. Reality isn't matching up with the expectations they've created in their heads. When this happens, you have a few choices: Step up and do everything you can to get reality to match your expectations. Change your expectations to meet the new reality. Or spend precious time and energy lamenting how unfair the world is and why this new reality is not your fault. It's not a black-and-white world, so I can say with confidence that the right answer probably lies somewhere between options one and two. What I can also tell you with complete confidence is that the last option will never get you anywhere. Yet I see it chosen every day. The option of excuses. The "if only" option. "If only I had done this or that." You didn't. It doesn't matter anymore. You shouldn't mind. Mind the future, not the past. What are you going to do to get back on your desired path?

In reality, the young should be the most resilient group out there. They have nothing but time and opportunity in front of them. That sudden curve in the road (not getting into the college of their choice or securing a prestigious internship) could actually be an exciting opportunity to change their trajectory (study something different, explore a different geography, save money at community college and then transfer).

But to a teen or twenty-something, a setback like that can be devastating. It most definitely matters to them, and they can't get past it. The "matter" becomes a barrier to success. And it's strictly mental. It will take self-discipline and perspective to move forward. To look at the long game and realize that they have way more time in front of them than behind. To accept the reality that they're the only one in control of how they think and act. No excuses, no regrets. Those things will anchor them to the past. If they want a different future, then they must think and act differently than they did in the past.

The mind is the most important tool we have. But it can also be a source of self-imposed limitations. Limitations and influences we are often unaware of that are working at the subconscious level. These are the cognitive biases we've discussed before and will continue to revisit. Again, cognitive bias, a concept introduced by Amos Tversky and Daniel Kahneman in the '70s and later expanded upon and popularized in their book *Thinking, Fast and Slow*, is the idea of systematic errors or faults in our thought processes that impact (usually negatively) our decision-making, choices, and perception of the world around us. A common cognitive bias is called the negativity bias or negativity effect. This is our natural tendency to give more attention and weight to the negative than the positive. We notice negatives more, even when they occur on an equal or lesser basis than positive events. There are differing explanations for why this occurs, but the most plausible seems to be rooted somewhere in the survival mechanisms of our caveman brain. For early humans, physical danger lurked around every corner, and we developed a natural attention to the things that could end our existence. Noticing the negative foremost became a survival instinct that still exists in the deep recesses of our subconscious and continues to influence us today.

If a student has been getting straight As on assignments and then gets a C, they tend to focus on the C and forget all the good work they've done. If a pitcher strikes out five batters in a row and the sixth batter jacks a home run, the home run is what we (and the pitcher) likely remember most. This subconscious draw to the negative can result in risk- and loss-averse behavior that freezes us up and prevents us from making good decisions or changing how we do things. Some ways to counter negativity bias are to take stock of your wins and accomplishments. Do it objectively. Write them down. Bring in an outside observer to objectively look at the list or make it with you. Take a pause, check yourself, and make an effort to look at the situation from a rational, data-informed perspective.

It isn't always the big things that bog us down. It's easy to get fixated on trivial matters and strengthen them from trivial to powerful. Counteracting that can be as simple as just not paying attention to those inconsequential distractions. If we make a concerted effort to ignore outside influences, they no long matter; ergo, they no longer have an impact on our mood, outlook, or demeanor.

Online reviews of a product or business are a classic example. I've seen business owners lose sleep over a negative Yelp review, despite having hundreds of good reviews. Sure, if the review is constructive criticism, learn from it. If not, just let it go. Better yet, don't even pay attention. Get your feedback directly from the customers that you interact with on a face-to-face basis. Everyone aims to have their business or product rated with five stars. But nothing is perfect and can be five stars to everyone. Take the negative in context with the positive, and attempt to look at things with an objective eye.

The most relevant application in today's society of "if you don't mind, it doesn't matter" is social media. If you're putting anything out there—whether it be tweets, a book, or God forbid something to do with politics, you had better be prepared for a high dose of negativity. I believe the prevailing vernacular, for lack of a better term, is "haters." They're unavoidable, so if you give them any credence, you're giving them life. If you don't care, if you don't even read the comments, then you can't mind. Joe Rogan had the best advice about social media: post it and forget it. By definition, others' opinions only matter if you let them.

Somewhere along the way, we seem to have forgotten the idea of "sticks and stones may break my bones, but words will never hurt me." Certain segments of our society now claim that words are as harmful as sticks and stones. It's simply not true. If someone hits you in the face with a stick, it's going to leave a bruise whether or not you want it to. Words, on the other hand, only hurt if you allow them to. I'm not saying that your feelings won't be injured or that a pointed insult might not sting, but how much it hurts and impacts you is within your control. The only thing that truly matters is your mind, and if you don't mind, it doesn't matter.

13

NOTHING LASTS FOREVER

Any other time and it would have been considered a pleasant Southern California night. The thermometer showed midsixties. The sky was clear with a light breeze—comfortable sweatshirt or light-jacket weather. It would have been the perfect opportunity for a Guinness on the patio of any number of different bars or restaurants in the San Diego area. Instead, I was lying on my back, nearly naked, on an icy steel pier jutting out from Naval Amphibious Base Coronado into Glorietta Bay. I, along with half of what was left of my BUD/S class, was shivering uncontrollably while an instructor sprayed a fine mist of water over us. I stared up into the sky wondering when this particular evolution would be over and what would be next.

My muscles began to involuntarily contract from the cold. Motor control was fading fast. Suddenly I was pulled back to reality by the yells of the instructor telling us to get back on our feet. We stood as quickly as possible, grateful to be able to move again and get the blood circulating.

Then it was our turn to get back into the water. The other half of the class had been floating next to the pier in water roughly the same temp as the air, using their trousers as floatation devices. The evolution called for you to take your pants off, tie each leg in a knot, flip them over your head to capture air, then quickly tie the waist off to create a floatation device you could slip your head through. If the air leaked out of your survival floatation, you had to slip it off your head and do it again. We completed the evolution and then helped the other half of the class out of the water so we could swap places.

At first the water actually felt warmer than the wet steel pier. That feeling didn't last long, and the cold rapidly seeped back in. Being immersed in cold water saps heat from the body relatively quickly, leading to uncontrollable shivering. I could barely form a thought, let alone speak a coherent sentence. Even consciousness started to fade. I had no clue how long we were in the water before again switching with the other half of the class. Our turn to freeze, lying on the steel pier again, swapping one cold hell for another.

The instructors had us do some jumping jacks and push-ups before instructing us, "On your back, gents. Don't want you to overheat with exercise. Heatstroke is serious business." Then one of the instructors, in a deadpan, mockingly sincere voice, continued voicing the concern we might be overheating. His solution was to spray us down with a hose.

"Would you like an Irish mist or a London fog?" he asked with a big grin on his face.

I couldn't tell you how long the evolution on the steel pier went on. It was all a blur. On the pier, in the water, back on the cold steel, back in the freezing water, again and again. Nearly every time we went back in the water, we were short another man. There were quite a few quitters that night. How did those that made it through to the next evolution and eventually on to graduate do it?

There isn't a definitive answer to that question, though many have tried to find it. If there were, I suppose we'd have the secret to graduating BUD/S. Some guys focused on making it day to day, meal to meal, event to event, or hour to hour. They utilized differing perspectives to help reach whichever milestone they identified, but the theme was the same: the pain and discomfort weren't going to last forever. Because nothing lasts forever.

In almost all situations, discomfort and pain are merely temporary obstacles. They will end, even though in the midst of those trials, it often becomes difficult to see that reality. Our minds jump ahead and make assumptions that the situation will continue on the same trajectory. We project our current state into the future as if nothing is going to change.

This simply isn't true. The only true constant is change. You've heard the clichéd saying that "the storm will pass." Well, it's true. The storm, devastating as it may be when you're in the middle of it, seeming like it will never end, will. As I write this chapter, the world is in the middle of a global pandemic storm. There is tragedy and death, uncertainty and confusion, anger and denial. Most people are going through a situation unlike anything they've ever been confronted with in their lives. We cannot know the future, but what we do know is that tomorrow will not be the same as today. Don't forget—the storm always passes.

That realization—or at least a partial understanding—got me though a lot of tough times in my career. But there is another, deeper meaning and different perspective of "nothing lasts forever" that took me years to appreciate. I had always viewed this concept as a way to get me through the tough times. It was there to remind me to endure, that there were clear skies ahead. It wasn't until later in life that I realized there was a flip side of that coin.

In 2006, about thirteen years into my career in the SEAL Teams and after a couple deployments to Afghanistan, a couple to Iraq, and coming off of a year of living and working out of Bahrain, I was afforded the opportunity to go to Monterey, California, to attend the Naval Postgraduate School. I had gotten married the month before leaving for Bahrain and had barely seen my new wife since we tied the knot. Going to school for my master's degree would be a welcome break. I'd get to spend some time with my wife while taking time to recover mind and body.

As I neared the end of my time at Monterey with a baby daughter as a new addition to the family, I started to think about what I was going to do next. I began talking with the SEAL detailer who would assign me my next job in the Teams. He was a prior boss of mine who knew me well and had been a great advocate in the past. He laid out a path that would bring me back to Naval Special Warfare Development Group in Dam Neck and do a year or so in operations before a two-year staff tour at JSOC (Joint Special Operations Command) at Fort Bragg, North Carolina. Hopefully, with the right timing and best-case scenario, I'd then return back to Dam Neck and take command of a squadron.

That path would be demanding but enjoyable and personally rewarding. It would demand sacrifice. It meant prioritizing work over family. It also meant that I would have an opportunity once again to work for and with the highest caliber of warriors on the planet, doing things that few in this world will ever experience.

There *was* an alternative that would be a more relaxed assignment. I was due for a joint staff tour (one of the boxes you have to check to move up in rank). This path would take me to one of the regional special operations commands called SOCSOUTH (Special Operations Command South) in southern Florida.

Every geographic region has a headquarters element that runs special operations in that region, and this was the one for South America. Depending on the current world situation and our foreign policy, each command carries with it a certain amount of priority and importance.

At the time, SOCSOUTH was not the premier place to go do a tour of duty. It wasn't involved with Afghanistan or Iraq and only tangentially related to the war on terror. It wasn't on the front-lines of confrontation with any of the other competitive global powers like Russia or China. That's not to say that nothing was happening in the region—Venezuela and Colombia were always hot spots—but it wasn't making headlines. In fact, SOCSOUTH was about the last place you'd want to go to advance your career and move up in rank. But the headquarters was in Homestead, Florida, and required significantly less travel (or so I thought). This would factor heavily in my decision.

I knew that if I took the path my old boss was laying out, I would be gone two hundred–plus days a year. I'd have to move my family at least three times in three years and would barely see my newborn girl. But I also knew that if I took it, not only would I be working at the pinnacle of special operations, but I would move up in rank and position and most likely get a command of my own, solidifying my path to making captain and maybe even admiral one day.

This is where the other side of the coin came into play. This time the things that wouldn't last forever weren't something negative or a hardship; they were the things I loved. It was about the idea that the good things in life also don't last forever.

There is one thing in this world that no amount of money can buy: time. Time is the most precious commodity that we have. You can't make more of it or get it back, so how you spend your time is the most important decision of your life.

I made the decision to prioritize my family over the navy and my career. I knew that my daughter wouldn't be a baby forever. I knew that I could never buy back the time that I would miss with her if I took the more kinetic path.

My father was also living in Fort Lauderdale at the time. By going to SOCSOUTH, I would have the opportunity to spend more time with him. It was the right decision for me, so I took it.

This isn't meant to put a value judgment on those who chose differently than I did. This was the choice that I made, to basically tank my career possibilities so that I could spend more time with my family. And I did it because I realized nothing lasts forever. Not the good times or the bad. I made sure to take advantage of the time when there wasn't a storm.

As it would turn out, it was the best decision I ever made. I was able to see my father a couple of times a month for most of my three years in Miami. I spent more time with him in those years than I had since high school. I still deployed to Colombia for six months (there was a war going on with the FARC, and there was the little matter of US hostages that had to be resolved) and went on smaller two- and three-week trips throughout the region on various jobs, but I was definitely home more than I was gone.

My father and I were able to play golf several times a month and spend holidays together. He got to know and spend time with his grandchildren and daughter-in-law. It was a perfect calm before the coming storm.

But as we know, nothing lasts forever. At the very end of my tour at SOCSOUTH, my father was diagnosed with liposarcoma, a rare and deadly cancer. For the next two years, the cancer would eat away at his body in the most horrific and painful way, eventually taking his life way too early. But nothing could take away the time that we got to spend together as a family during those years.

This story isn't meant to be sad or depressing. In fact, it's a happy story. My kids still remember their pop-pop fondly. I often reflect back on the parties and meals at his house, the time spent on his boat cruising the canals of Fort Lauderdale. The many golf outings, the smile on his face as he played with his grandkids. Today I'm thankful that we had that time together.

The ability to look ahead and see yourself in a situation other than the one you're currently in is not innate. And then to make life decisions based not on what you are currently experiencing but what could happen in the future is particularly daunting. If anything, it's counterintuitive and a learned skill. It's tantamount to looking into a crystal ball, when reason tells us that is impossible. As humans we're wired to focus on our current predicament, whether it's positive or negative. That can make it difficult to look up and out.

The first step is to be aware of that limited picture. Try not to emotionally react to what's going on around you. Instead, think critically and objectively about what the same scenario will look like down the line. In a day, a week, a month, a year. In some cases, it's as simple as consciously thinking, "This will not last forever," whatever *this* is. From there it's an easy leap to see into a window with an alternate future and make present decisions based on that information. Because nothing lasts forever.

It's human nature to assume that whatever trajectory we are on will remain constant. But remember, the only constant is change. If the stock market is going up, you can be assured that at some point it will go down. Yet when housing prices increase, the market sees an influx of home purchases. It's hard for a buyer to separate the current climate from what makes historical sense: that any market will always even off and dip eventually. The trajectory of anything—a market, our emotions, success at work—charts more like rolling hills than a straight, inclining (or declining) line. In fact, our entire societal structure is designed to regress to the mean. Our political system, in theory, has a series of checks and balances built into it. In short, what goes up is supposed to come back down. Even when it doesn't seem like it will.

When things at work are going well, it's hard to imagine them going poorly. You get a raise, win a big contract, get kudos from the boss. It's hard to place yourself in the opposite scenario.

The inverse holds true as well. And because of those cognitive blinders, we often don't build in proper protections or insurances. Not enough of us put aside money for a "rainy day fund" when the economy is good, or run a marathon before our bodies break down, or backpack across Europe before having kids. We think our current circumstance will last forever. They won't. That's why it's so important to take advantage of the fair weather between the storms to make gains.

There are debates as to whom to credit with the saying "Youth is wasted on the young," but no matter who said it, I buy the melancholic sentiment. When I tell my kids how good they have it, they look at me cross-eyed. Yes, I tell them, you should appreciate such a carefree life with no responsibilities. This should be the best time of your life! But like all adolescents, preteen angst makes it hard to believe their old man. I never believed it when I was young. I was too wrapped up in my current life of friends, girls, sports, and school to contemplate a future with bills, achy muscles, and traffic.

My parents did more than just advise me to enjoy my youth; they made sure I did. In fact, their actions proved they subscribed to the idea of nothing lasting forever.

Before my dad reached the peak of his success, he got transferred to Colorado. We weren't poor, but we certainly weren't rich either. But it was important to them that my siblings and I learned to ski, and we took advantage of the amazing slopes in Colorado, even if it meant putting my parents in some debt. Trips, equipment, lift tickets—they weren't cheap, but my parents knew that being in debt wouldn't last forever, nor would living in Colorado. So they embraced some temporary discomfort, knowing it wouldn't last, to take advantage of a limited opportunity. I'm certainly grateful that they did.

We've talked about how businesses must adapt or fail. There is no staying the same. Kodak, Polaroid, Myspace—all had great success, but they ultimately failed because they didn't subscribe to the theory that nothing lasts forever.

Kodak was one of the most successful companies in the world right up until the moment it wasn't. The amazing thing was that Kodak saw the disruptive change of the digital world coming and still was unable to capitalize on it. Ultimately, they couldn't get away from the idea of printing film, their core business, which had remained largely unchanged for years.

Similarly, Polaroid couldn't accept the idea that nothing lasts forever either. Their leadership was in complete shock when it became apparent to them (too late) that people no longer wanted hard copies of all their photos. From 2001 to 2009, Polaroid filed bankruptcy twice and from 2005 to 2009 went through six CEOs. Polaroid was unable to envision the massive disruption of the storm of the digital transformation and continued to make decisions based on the underlying assumption that the trajectory of printed photos would remain the same. Countless companies now exist as only shadows of their former selves or as case studies for up-and-coming MBAs, cautionary tales on how to *not* evolve. Embracing the idea that nothing lasts forever would have served them well.

The same holds true when starting a new business. Ask any entrepreneur about the workload for a startup. Sixteen- and eighteen-hour days, working weekends, barely seeing their family. But most understand that pace will not last forever. It's a means to an end: once the business is established, the owner can pull back a little. He or she can hire more employees and enjoy the fruits of their labor.

It's the same with a new job. There's always a learning curve when tackling anything new. You may get frustrated and feel like you're drinking from the proverbial fire hose. But this too shall pass. As you gain more experience, your past confusion will be a distant memory. You'll continue to perfect your craft until you can hardly remember the earlier difficulties.

Short-term memory can be an aid when utilizing the

nothing-lasts-forever mantra. Evolution has done a good job of allowing us to forget the hardships that come along with bringing a new life into the world. The morning sickness of pregnancy and sleepless nights of new parenthood seem insurmountable when a family is in the throes of them, but when your toddler is laughing and giving you hugs, those painful memories seem like they happened to someone else. This is by evolutionary design—if we remembered how hard having children is, we might not be as apt to do it again. And when you're in the middle of a temper tantrum or sleep regression, it's hard to imagine your second-grader smiling on the first day of school or your son's first hit in baseball. But those days will come.

There's an element of self-sacrifice that comes with this philosophy. It's about looking to the future and understanding that what you do today will have a profound impact on what happens to you moving forward. It's about overcoming today's challenges to better your future prospects.

That could be as simple as maxing out your 401(k). When you're younger, living a more austere life demonstrates your willingness for self-sacrifice with an eye to retirement, no matter how distant that day may seem. Any money you save now will compound significantly by the time you're ready to retire. You understand that eating ramen noodles in a six-hundred-square-foot apartment won't last forever and will lead to a higher quality of life in the future. The hard work and expense of medical school can be a painful pill to swallow for a decade or more, but you know that by putting in the work, your future will be brighter.

The death of a loved one is a painful experience that unfortunately we all go through at some point. One some levels, that pain will never fully go away. But it will get better. The pain in that moment won't last forever. Think of the millions of people who have gone through the same thing and are living happy lives. Fundamentally, I believe we all understand that eventually we will come to terms and get over the loss, even if it doesn't seem like it in the moment.

Remember, "nothing lasts forever" applies to good times and bad. In the good, take the time to appreciate those moments with one eye on the horizon and a mind toward preparing for the storm that is sure to come. And when you find yourself in that storm, take solace in the fact that there is always a silver lining in the clouds and clear skies somewhere ahead. Remind yourself that nothing lasts forever.

14

NEVER QUIT

The most famous phrase associated with the SEAL Teams is probably "never quit." I have no idea who first coined it, but it's another one of those sayings that was instilled in me before I even began BUD/S.

In fact, if there is any "secret" to getting through BUD/S, it's to simply never quit. You push until you think you can't take another step or lie for another second in the cold Pacific. Then you push a little more. You do one more push-up, one more pull-up, take one more step, spend one more second in the cold water. Unless you are unconscious or dead, you *can* keep going. You run until you can't run, then you walk until you can't walk, then you crawl until you can't crawl. Just keep pushing forward.

The phrase and idea go back to well before the SEAL Teams—probably before the written word. Survivors and winners have been repeating this mantra for generations for a reason: it's true, and it works.

If we look to the extremes, to actual life-and-death situations, it's often the difference between one and the other. Under duress, immense pain, or impossible odds, the easiest path—the path of least resistance—is to give up. It's more difficult to fight to the last breath. But that's exactly what you must do in order to not only survive but thrive. Dylan Thomas famously wrote, "Do not go gentle into that good night. Rage, rage against the dying of the light." That quote is memorable for a reason. In fact, I'd argue that all incredible stories of survival and adventure share this maxim. You don't read the stories of those who rolled over and gave up.

Never quitting is about failing. It's about getting knocked down and then getting up to do it over again. Putting one foot in front of the other. Taking one more swim stroke or kick of the fins. One more breath, one more heartbeat. It's about not giving in when all seems lost. Most people fundamentally understand the concept of never quitting, or at least the "what" aspect of it. Fewer know how—and when—to apply it.

Like all the maxims in this book, there is more to never quitting than what's on the surface. It doesn't mean that if you merely keep doing what you're doing, everything will work out no matter what. Success isn't simply a function of continuing down the same path without stopping. It's not about doing the same thing over and over and expecting different results. That, of course, is the definition of insanity.

Persistence alone is not enough. You must have persistence with purpose. Persistence with deliberate thought. That means you need to follow a vector or a general azimuth. You must have a belief in what you're doing and a passion to continue doing it.

Persistence without passion or conviction is hollow. If you don't *truly* want something, it will be extremely difficult to persist through adversity. You must have a true craving to reach your desired future. This could be a near future, like the next step up the mountain. Or the far future, like reaching the summit. It could also be a farther future, like summiting the highest peaks on each continent. But a desired future provides directionality and purpose to your efforts.

That being said, there is also a time when letting go is the right thing to do.

A plethora of variables and unknowns come into play when human beings and their emotions and goals are involved. While staying the course and not giving up are usually admirable traits, there are instances when moving on is the right course of action. What isn't always clear is when that time is right, or even the difference between quitting and moving on.

The difference between the two is rooted in your intention and motivation. Quitting is when you stop doing something because it's too hard, even when you have the desire to continue. Letting go occurs when your desire is truly gone or when continuing would do more harm than good. Either the end goal is no longer important, or it would be detrimental. If you stop because it hurts to go on, that's quitting. If the path you're on will hurt you in the long run, that's moving on. Quitting ends in regret. Moving on leads to a fresh start.

Let's say you're training for a marathon. You're getting up early and running each morning, and then on the weekends going for longer runs. But it's hard to get out of bed before you have to every morning. It's not fun. You'd rather go to wineries or relax at home on the weekends. So you decide to stop training and withdraw from the race.

I think we'd all agree that's quitting. The day of the marathon, my guess is you'd have some regrets about not being there. In hindsight, you might wish you had continued training. Were those extra hours in bed worth it? Only you can decide that.

Now let's say you tore your ACL training for the marathon. I don't think anyone would argue that you should push forward and go through with the race. You'd do more harm to your body than good. That's not quitting. That's understanding circumstances change. You may still be bummed on race day, but you won't regret your actions or decision.

When the situation or circumstances would result in something positive but you are too lazy or afraid to pursue it, it's quitting. If something is having a negative impact on you, letting go and moving on takes strength and courage.

A good example of this—and how it isn't black or white—is in relationships.

If you're in an abusive relationship, the equation is easy: leaving the abusive person isn't quitting whatsoever; it's putting yourself in a better, healthier situation. Contrarily, if you are in a twenty-year marriage with young children and you decide to leave and get a divorce after a minor argument, it's quitting. But sometimes it isn't as simple—there is middle ground.

The very nature of relationships means there will be ups and downs to navigate. Relationships are hard work, and like anything, if you're not willing to put in the work, they won't succeed. If you end a relationship just because you don't want to put in the work, then that might be quitting. How much work should you put in? Are there more good times or bad? Ending a relationship is one of the hardest decisions anyone has to make.

Is doing so abandoning what you have or moving on to greener pastures? Time will tell: Down the road, do you think you will regret ending it?

It's the same with your career. If you're miserable at work, should you throw in the towel and quit? Would it be better for you to find another job or start your own business? I think it's important to look at why you're miserable in the current situation.

Is it a toxic environment? Are there legal, moral, or ethical issues? If so, then it's safe to say it's time to move on. Is it a job that you enjoy but the hours are long and the demands are high? If you left, would it be because the work took too much effort? Would you look back fondly at your time with the company and regret moving to a more low-pressure role somewhere else? Are the rewards worth the effort? Will you be as fulfilled or make as much money doing something easier? All these questions must be answered when analyzing the data and making a decision.

You can't look at the world in absolutes. Every situation and challenge are different. Stopping something you're doing does not always mean you failed. It doesn't necessarily mean you quit. The majority of the time, I subscribe to the "never quit" mentality, but there is a danger in being absolutist. There's something to be said for taking a more flexible point of view.

We spend resources, money, time, effort, and emotion on all sorts of endeavors. Once spent, usually those resources are not recoverable. We should be careful to not let these sunk costs anchor and drag us down in the name of "never quit." Sometimes the right move is to cut your losses, let go, and not continue down the spiral of absolutist thinking. Sometimes it's about being able to fight another day. It takes enormous courage and mental fortitude to realize when that time has come and a lot of wisdom to know the difference between quitting and moving on.

It takes toughness, dedication, and bravery to climb Mount Everest. People spend hundreds of thousands of dollars and train for years in an attempt to reach the summit. They travel from all over the world and pledge to themselves that they will brave the elements and not quit in order to meet their goal. But a lot of lives have been lost on that mountain because people weren't brave or tough enough to stop and move on from their climb. They refused to take other data points into account when deciding whether to quit or keep going, and they ended up dying because of it. This obsession with achieving their goal forced them to ignore external factors like timing, weather conditions, and congestion on the mountain.

Circumstances and the environment can also dictate whether ceasing an activity falls under giving up or letting go. When on an op in the SEAL Teams, much of the criteria above would have suggested halting a mission was acceptable. Needless to say, that never happened. The stakes dictated that. There are no time-outs or do-overs in war. It didn't matter what happened; we were going to complete the mission. Torn ACLs or a sacrifice/reward analysis didn't come into play.

I remember a particularly grueling mission in Afghanistan where the never-quit mentality was displayed in full force. We had been inserted by helos on the side of a mountain twelve thousand feet high. It had such a vertical face that our helo hadn't even been able to put its wheels down—we just had to jump out into the night and try not get dragged down the mountain by our rucks.

I was carrying one hundred pounds of equipment that I'd have to haul a thousand feet straight up the mountain to set up an observation post overlooking key terrain across the valley below us. The steep hike up the mountain would be incredibly rough.

We started our climb, and it wasn't long before my legs and lungs were on fire. The air was incredibly thin (that's why the helos couldn't take us the whole way up—their rotors couldn't keep the bird aloft in such thin air), so it was hard to catch your breath. I'd take two or three steps and collapse, then get up and do it again. Over and over. I puked three times on the way up. It was a total gut check, but there was no choice. You couldn't quit. You couldn't go back. We were making it to the top of that mountain no matter what. It took us four or five hours, but we made it.

It was the same when we were in the boats on a rough ocean. It might have been an all-night transit with our necks and verte-brae getting bounced around for eight hours. Our backs would get beat to hell as the boat was slammed by waves for hours on end. We might be throwing up and peeing blood when we were done, but no one was like, "It's too rough, let's go back." The environment and circumstances dictated that response. We couldn't allow ourselves to give in to the pain. Now, if there were the same conditions on a fishing trip, you'd be stupid to keep going. Catching tuna is not worth peeing blood and having lifelong back pain. The stakes are different. Environment is an important variable to include in your internal algorithm.

There's also an element of threshold. Everyone's is different, and everyone's experience pushing through pain and discom-fort varies. Getting smashed on a boat all night is not something most people are able to take, even in a wartime setting. But we had been trained to be able to take it. That's what BUD/S is designed to do: find those who can take it, and then train them to function while doing so. As we've seen with all our mantras, these traits need to be honed. Practiced and perfected. There is no real-world BUD/S for people who want to train themselves to perform under pain, stress, and pressure, but there are certainly ways to get your body and mind more apt to never quit.

There are plenty of reports about the benefit of cold showers: increased heart rate, strengthening of the immune system, boosted mood, and anti-inflammatory properties are a few. But you know what? Cold showers suck. No one *wants* to take a cold shower. So why take one?

Because, aside from the health benefits, they can also be good training to develop that never-quit attitude. If you can suck it up and stand under some cold water when it's uncomfortable and not jump out, maybe you can stick through the next difficult situation life throws at you. Maybe that's why we spend so much time in cold water in BUD/S.

Don't start with twenty-minute cold showers—start with two minutes, and then work your way up to five. Check out the writings and ideas of Wim Hof, a Dutch athlete and Guinness World Record holder, or Ben Greenfield, fitness coach and biohacker, for some more specific ideas on the benefits and ways to use cold water in your training. Set a goal, and follow through with it. Just don't quit. Do it every day for, say, a month. See if you can manage—it will be good training for other obstacles life throws at you.

Identify and seek out things that make you uncomfortable but you know are good for your long-term development. Embrace one of them. Look for things that don't provide immediate gratification. This could be something physical. If pull-ups are hard for you to do, find a pull-up program online, set a goal of twenty, and don't quit until you've achieved it.

It could be something mental. Maybe you don't enjoy or are afraid of public speaking. Vow to give presentations at work. Join a public-speaking organization like Toastmasters. Try something small, get some wins under your belt, and progress from there.

But no matter how prepared, how tough you are, there will be times when the right thing to do is cut your losses and move on. A lot of times, the challenge will be the timing. Knowing when it's time to get out of an investment, look for a new job, start a business, make an acquisition, or end/begin a relationship. It's the difference between quitting and moving on.

There's the old example of a boxer who unretires one too many times and ends up punch-drunk. It's happening in the NFL right now: guys like Andrew Luck and Calvin Johnson retiring while still young and relatively healthy. The timing equation for them is different than it was for players in past generations. They've made enough money and have additional opportunities that allow them to retire young. They aren't quitting or giving up—it's just the right time for them to move on. We all have these decisions to make in our lives.

When I was in college, my scholarship put me on a path to being commissioned in the Marine Corps. I soon realized that wasn't the path I wanted to be on. I wanted to join the navy to become a SEAL. Switching from the marine option to the navy option wasn't an easy course change. Pursuing my passion and moving on from the marines looked like quitting to the Marine Corps staff. I became alienated from them while also not fitting in with the navy side of the house. I would have to endure over a year and a half of living in limbo between the two, with both sides unhappy and throwing major obstacles in my path. I was told outright that I would never make it to the SEAL Teams. I was put under a microscope. Both sides looked for any excuse to get rid of me and make my life miserable. I endured physical and mental hazing from Marine Corps and navy staff and students. None of it mattered. I knew the direction I wanted to go. I persisted with purpose. There would be absolutely no short-term gratification, but I never quit pursuing the long term vector of becoming a SEAL.

I have a general guideline for my kids: if they start a sport, they have to complete the season. Doesn't matter if the practices are hard or they aren't getting playing time. They don't have to play again next year if they don't want to, but they have to see that season through. I don't want them to think that quitting is OK. They won't be harmed in the long run by staying on the team, and I'd like to think they'd regret it if they quit.

I said "general guideline" rather than "rule." Remember, the world isn't black and white. Absolutes can short-circuit our ability to be flexible and change direction with the circumstances.

There was one time I allowed my son to quit his soccer team. Correction—I pulled him off the team. The coach was so bad and the environment so toxic, I decided that staying on that team and finishing the season would do him more harm than good. In this case, he didn't quit the team; he moved on. This is where judgment comes into play. Was there going to be a negative impact if he stopped playing soccer? We decided that not only would there not be a negative impact if he left the team, there would actually be a positive one. That's the difference.

The other main difference when determining if it's quitting or letting go harkens back to the pain versus discomfort analysis. If something is painful, depending on circumstances, environment, and timing, it's probably a good idea to stop. If it's merely uncomfortable and will lead to a greater good, it's time to adopt that never-quit attitude. It might be difficult and suck, but in the long run, it will be worth the sacrifice. In the end, only you can make that decision.

15

SLOW IS SMOOTH, SMOOTH IS FAST

It was just after ten a.m. I was standing at the edge of the pool (or, as the instructors called it, the combat training tank) on Naval Amphibious Base Coronado. That morning my class had already completed an hour and half of calisthenics on the grinder at the BUD/S compound, run four miles in soft sand along the beach, and run the mile or so to the pool with fins and mask in hand.

We were waiting for the order to jump into the water and begin the next evolution. Like every student, I had my feet tied together, hands tied behind my back, swim mask on. The evolution we were about to undertake was called drownproofing, designed to test our comfort in the water. To see if we could stay in control and maintain our composure under less-than-desirable circumstances. Above all else, we needed to avoid panicking.

The task began with jumping into the nine-foot depth portion of the pool and letting out just enough air to allow us to slowly sink. When we hit the bottom, we were supposed to flex our knees and slowly push off with just enough force to propel us back to the surface. We needed to maintain just enough momentum to get a breath and then start the process over. If you got in a smooth rhythm, it could be a relatively easy and relaxing exercise. If you didn't, you were in for a real bad day.

After a while, the instructors upped the ante. They made us do a front flip underwater, which was particularly difficult to achieve with our hands tied behind our backs. It takes up energy, uses more air, and interrupts your smooth breathing cycle. As you complete the flip, your momentum slows, and you need to let out more air to reach the bottom. Instinct tells you to get another breath as fast as possible. The temptation is to push off the bottom as hard as you can and torpedo out of the water. But if you do that, your time above the water is shorter than if you had calmly pushed off the bottom and maintained a smooth rhythm. It will leave you rocketing back to the bottom and repeating the cycle. After a few flips, you find your lungs on fire and the very scary feeling of not getting enough air.

These are all distractions. Noise. If you succumbed to the noise, you might try to tread water. You'd struggle and eventually make your way to the side of the pool. Fail.

Or you could stay calm and get back in sync. You could ignore your lungs burning and keep your rhythm. With each trip to the surface, they would burn a little less. Soon we were back in the comfort zone, just in time for the instructors to throw us for the next loop. Now we had to pick our masks up from the bottom of the pool with our teeth. Breathing was interrupted again, and holding the mask in our mouths prevented us from opening wide and getting a good breath when we surfaced. Instead we had to start breathing through our nose. Our lungs were again on fire. But those who stayed calm and slowed down remained smooth. We needed to make our actions deliberate rather than reactionary to cut through the noise.

Slow is smooth, smooth is fast. It's another one of those common sayings at BUD/S and throughout the Teams. I'm sure it means different things to different people, but to me, it always reminded me to pay attention to the basics, cut through the noise, and to be thoughtful and deliberate in my actions.

I hear a lot of critiques about this maxim. "How can slow be fast? That doesn't make any sense. Slow is slow and fast is fast." OK, I get it. There are a lot of linear thinkers out there. The problem is, the world we live in and most of the challenges we confront are not linear. They often demand a different approach, so bear with me. Like nearly every other maxim I've talked about in this book, it's not meant to be taken literally. There are nuances to it. The dichotomy should make you think about it in a deliberate manner.

The way that I like to interpret "slow is smooth, smooth is fast" is in stressing the mastery of the fundamentals. The synthesis of individual parts to make something seamless and smooth, whether it's a task, problem, exercise, or movement. It's a cumulative effort where the sum is truly greater than the parts.

When you watch elite athletes—those at the top of their game— they have a different look about them. They make it—whatever *it* is—seem easy. They possess such a mastery of the fundamentals and how the game and their bodies work that hitting a ball or skiing down a mountain appears smooth and effortless.

Think about Usain Bolt running a race. Does he appear to be

working harder or expending more energy than his opponents as he rips past them? Or does he look smooth and effortless? It's the latter, of course; his skill and natural ability allow him to be energy efficient. There is little wasted motion. That skill comes from mastering the basic parts of running and implementing them cumulatively. The correct stride length, head placement, pumping arms, and leg-push all work together in a harmonious motion that propels him forward faster than anyone else, while he simultaneously appears cool and natural. That's because at that level, Bolt has mastered each element of sprinting and is innately able to apply them synchronously. Remember, whatever the domain, slow is smooth, smooth is fast begins with the fundamentals.

It's the same with a golf swing. The best golfers have beautiful, effortless swings. Poor golfers look out of rhythm. It's because they haven't perfected the fundamentals or brought the individual parts together to create a greater whole. And the end result is an ugly golf swing and a shank into the water. Go look up some videos on YouTube and watch Fred Couples swing a golf club, then look up Charles Barkley's swing, and you'll know exactly what I'm talking about.

I was fortunate to have a background in swimming when I got to BUD/S. I was no phenom or collegiate swimmer, but I swam competitively up until high school, which gave me a good foundation for stroke technique and how the body moves through the water. Again, I wasn't a master, but I was 80–90 percent there, and having that base meant I was one of the fastest swimmers in my class.

I would see other guys putting out five times the effort I was yet going way slower. You'd watch them slapping their hands, beating up the water, creating a lot of motion and burning tons of energy, but because they didn't have a mastery of the techniques, they weren't able to go as fast. They didn't understand the fundamentals: they didn't know how to get their body horizontal in the water, of the importance of rolling their hips or keeping their head down and body streamlined. They'd have their head angled up and chest pushing water, which meant they had to expend ten times as much energy as I did to accomplish the same thing.

Being smooth is about not rushing an activity or thought. When you do that, energy is wasted, and the last thing that you will be is smooth. All that effort and franticness is counterproductive. It's about being efficient, and the only way you can do that is to master the basic techniques of your field.

Take something as simple as typing. There are widely accepted best practices when it comes to efficiently typing on a QWERTY keyboard. Index fingers on *f* and *j*. Pinkies on semicolon and *a*. Thumbs on the spacebar. The basics. And if you don't have those basics down, you'll never be a fast typist. Yet someone who is hunting and pecking can look like they're moving a mile a minute while only typing fifteen words a minute. But a stenographer's fingers glide over the keyboard gracefully and with minimal motion, banging out a hundred words a minute. Once you master the fundamentals, you can begin perfecting your technique.

Each obstacle in the obstacle course at BUD/S has a specific strategy for quickly completing it, a trick or technique that helps students go through it efficiently. If you watch students tackling the course, you can tell the difference between those muscling through it with brute force and those using technique to clear each obstacle smoothly. The ones moving through it smoothly go faster. They might not be using as much frenetic motion and can actually appear to be going slower, but they finish it quicker by not fighting themselves or the obstacle.

This concept exists in everything we do. Understanding the fundamentals, mastering those parts, and then putting them together as a single system. It's not enough to merely master the parts; you have to recognize that they're part of a larger system, and then they have to go together.

Like so many of our mantras, it's about embracing the counterintuitive approach. With this maxim, that contradiction is in the title. But it's not about being slow. It means being deliberate and thoughtful to allow you to have a rhythm and be smooth in your efforts. That is where the efficiency and speed come from. It's an economy of movement, force, and energy that allows you to go farther and faster.

In business, that smoothness comes from deliberate thought. Daniel Kahneman breaks it down well in his book *Thinking, Fast and Slow*. He talks about two basic types of thinking: automatic and deliberate. Automatic thinking is intuitive and reactionary and is usually lower quality. It is thinking that is often driven by lessons derived from previous experience with a problem or situation. This type of thinking merely suffices. It's not optimal, but it is usually good enough.

Your brain naturally gravitates toward this type of thinking. It's necessary for us to conserve energy and not overthink everything. Our brains try to move a lot of what we think into this realm. Muscle memory engages the automatic-thinking side of the brain. We develop standard operating procedures (SOPs) or emergency procedures to remove the slower, deliberate process of thinking into the automatic realm. Automatic thinking is absolutely necessary to our survival and happens subconsciously. Think of it as the operating system of the computer that is always running in the background. If I ask you what two plus two is, you will respond "four" without hesitation. You automatically hit your brakes if you see a car in front of you come to a stop. Automatic thinking is passive and always present. However, that type of thinking is easily influenced and tricked by cognitive biases and logical fallacies. In general, it's not sufficient for tackling multifaceted issues.

Deliberate thinking is slower and harder but also higher quality. It requires more energy, attention, and an understanding of the fundamentals. But it is how to best deal with complex problems. Deliberate thinking allows us to make multilevel comparisons, take into consideration data and statistical analysis, and connect seemingly distant concepts and ideas. It's about appreciating the parts and pieces of the issue and how they fit together as a system. Deliberate thinking is the supporting characteristic to the ever-present automatic thinking for situations or problems that contain a high level of complexity or uncertainty.

Let's say you're deciding whether or not to take on financing or make an acquisition for your company. It's important to think critically and deliberately, examining and understanding the fundamentals of the deal. Automatic thinking—just doing something because that's the way it's always been done or that's what you did last time and it worked—can fool you and lead you down the wrong path. You need to start by examining each situation at its core and going back to the basics of business. Ask yourself, "What's the cash flow? What's the value?" Only after analyzing the basics can you begin to make an educated decision.

You often see this now with technology companies. Investors can overlook the fundamentals. Many of these companies have no profits, yet they're hot and sexy in the market, and people are eager to invest in them. But that automatic thinking has led to a lot of collapses and money lost in that sector. The fundamentals get ignored: value, cash flow, and what the real business is.

As you use and hone these critical thinking skills, you will make better decisions. As you practice them and do it more, you'll get better and better at it. It's the same idea as breaking down your golf swing or swimming stroke. Ask yourself, "What are the fundamental pieces of this?" Constantly ask, "Why? Why is this happening? What am I missing?" When you aren't asking these questions, you're in automatic-thinking mode.

Automatic thinking just leads to doing the same things the same way. It's how people get bogged down by pedigrees and place an undue emphasis on titles. If you break it down to the basics, why do companies hire Harvard MBAs? At the core, it's because they assume those candidates are smart. And yes, to get an MBA from Harvard, you must be smart. But the degree alone does not automatically make someone smarter than somebody else with an MBA from Boston University. Dig deeper. Ask the tough questions. Don't just assume intelligence based on a degree. It's when you direct focused energy and attention on what's below the surface that you are able to make efficient and proper decisions.

Similarly, company boards regularly hire retired admirals and generals simply due to their military title. I'd argue that often critical-thinking skills are not being used to make those hires. Companies are fooled by a bias or logical fallacy of appeal to authority. Just because someone has the title of admiral or general does not mean they are competent. Believe me, I know. It simply means they've worked their way up through the bureaucracy of a largely political system to get to a point where they've reached such a rank. Yet many of these boards assign an overvaluation to these titles and end up hiring them based on a single intuitive thought process. Often they don't look further than the title. They don't ask themselves the basic questions of hiring: What did they do in the military? What were they running? What successes did they have? How did they lead? The title may be a factor in a deliberate hiring process, and it certainly doesn't preclude them from being a strong candidate, but it shouldn't be the end-all, be-all.

It comes back to employing deliberate-thinking strategies in order to understand and master the fundamentals. That will lead to smoothness, efficiency, and speed. If you don't execute the basic concepts of whatever domain you're operating within, it's impossible to be smooth. You'll make intuitive decisions misguided by biases and logical fallacies. When you hear "Harvard" or "Yale" or "admiral" or "general" and your intuitive internal response is, "That person must be really competent," it's a reaction. The thoughtful response would be, "That's interesting. Let me dig deeper and figure out all the pieces that come with this person." The smoother you are with your thinking, the higher quality your decisions will be.

That isn't to say this is easy to do. Asking these questions and thinking more deeply is frustrating. It's easier to say, "Hire the dude from Harvard." But that's reactionary thinking. It's not always the right answer. Sometimes you have to put intuition in check. It doesn't necessarily mean your intuition is incorrect, but it does mean you have to deliberately think through those assumptions and examine them at the most basic level. Only by going deeper will you respond to your environment rather than react to it.

Think of any competition against another person or team. Part of a good strategy is to get your opponent to react. Faking a shot in basketball, putting the queen in check in chess, leading with a jab in a boxing match—they're all meant to get your rival off balance. Knee-jerk reactions will lead to worse decisions, which is what we want our opponent to do.

It's the same with deception campaigns in warfare and politics. They're designed to get people to react with low-quality thinking rather than responding to the environment and deliberately thinking through the situation to be smooth and fast.

We also do it to ourselves. It's easy to take the path of least resistance instead of thinking critically and examining our thoughts and actions for efficiency. Are you only doing something because that's the way it's always been done? If so, I would advise breaking the scenario down to its fundamentals and building it back up analytically.

This comes into play with how we handle time management. It's all too common to expend a lot of energy without being productive. Look at how some companies handle meetings: What are they trying to achieve with them? Are meetings an efficient use of everyone's time? Are they even necessary in the first place? Is the goal of the meeting to share information or to elicit a decision? Smoothness or efficiency is only going to come from thinking critically about how best to spend your time.

This too has both mental and physical applications. We spent a lot of time on the fundamentals of drawing a pistol in the SEAL Teams so when the time came to use that weapon, we were smooth, fast, and deadly.

There are many parts of being efficient with a holstered pistol, and they all have to work in concert. If one of the fundamentals breaks down, it's going to be a bad day. Your hand travels down the side of your body, thumb pushed down and slightly forward. You release the thumb break as the web of your hand contacts the grip, fingers wrapped around it, beginning to pull the pistol from the holster. As soon as the weapon clears leather, your wrist and lower arm rotate the pistol to a horizontal position, and you immediately point it at the target, finger moving over the trigger as your off hand comes to complete the grip, the pistol rises, and the trigger is squeezed to its break point as the sights match up to eye level and the round is fired. All this occurs in under a second. All of it working as a smooth, unified system rather than individual movements in order to be done fast.

Another important aspect of firearms training is the magazine (the device that holds your ammunition rounds or cartridges—please don't call it a clip) change, both for a pistol and rifle. If you're in a firefight or a shooting competition, a smooth magazine change is crucial. We practiced magazine changes in all our weapons systems constantly. In competition, you lose valuable time when you're not shooting, and in combat you're defenseless. A magazine change requires depressing a release button to drop the empty magazine from the weapon. At the same time, you are reaching for a full magazine from wherever you have it stored on your kit and inserting it into the magazine well. If you rush and fumble when grabbing the new magazine or have it facing the wrong way and don't insert it smoothly, you lose precious seconds. A well-trained shooter is smooth in their mag change, not rushed or frazzled. They will have practiced the maneuver so many times that it's the automatic-thinking side of their brain executing, but the work to get there was done by the deliberate side during training.

I knew exactly where my spare magazines were located on my kit. If I had changed configurations, I would have had to go back to deliberate thinking and practice developing the muscle memory of the new location in order to get back to being smooth and fast.

This is the key to everything we do, whether it's athletics, closing a sale, or some other complex problem. Use deliberate thinking to start with, and don't rush or get frazzled. Take your time. It could be as short as an extra heartbeat or breath, or as long as days or weeks, depending on the situation. As we rush or get hurried beyond our capabilities, mistakes happen. Mistakes tend to compound quickly, and you may soon find yourself making more mistakes or needing to start over.

The next time you find yourself in unfamiliar territory or feeling rushed, repeat to yourself the mantra "Slow is smooth, smooth is fast" as a reminder to be deliberate. I guarantee the results will speak for themselves.

16

IF YOU'RE NOT CHEATING, YOU'RE NOT TRYING

This is another saying that didn't originate in the SEAL Teams but was very popular when I was active, despite higher head-quarters' efforts to stamp it out. They did everything they could to purge it from our ethos and culture, though I don't know how successful they were. I certainly still heard it echoing in the halls when I was on active duty. Whether or not it still exists today, I couldn't tell you, but I suspect it does in some form or another.

SEALs are taught to exploit every possible advantage, whether in training or combat. We were always looking for an edge. We had no interest in meeting the enemy with parity or symmetry. We wanted outsized asymmetric advantages, and we did every-thing we could to ensure we had them.

The philosophy of "if you're not cheating, you're not trying" seemed to surge in popularity throughout professional sports and athletics in the '70s, '80s, and '90s. Richard Petty, the famous NASCAR driver, Mark Grace of the Chicago Cubs, and San Francisco 49ers quarterback Joe Montana all publicly embraced some version of the saying. They used the common justification that since everyone is trying to gain some sort of edge to win in competition, they needed to push (and often exceed) the boundaries of the rules.

Several large-scale cheating scandals leading to severe punishments over the past decade-plus have shined a light on what seems to be perceived as prevalent cheating across professional sports. While a harsh stigma has since developed that shames perceived cheaters, I don't think anyone believes cheating no longer happens. More sophisticated schemes have just developed. It used to be wide receivers putting Stickum on their hands, linemen spraying silicone on their jerseys, pitchers scuffing baseballs, and batters corking bats. That doesn't include the wide prevalence of performance-enhancing drugs throughout all sports—steroids, amphetamines, blood doping, and so on. Even businessmen and students aren't immune, whether it's amphetamines on Wall Street or nootropics ("smart drugs") in offices, classrooms, and research laboratories.

While many of those cheating methods have been publicized and countermeasures to catch offenders implemented, it would be foolish to think today's athletes aren't finding new methods to push the rules. Look at the Houston Astros—they were just implicated in a huge cheating scandal when it was discovered they were using electronics to steal signs. In a competitive environment with limited rewards and resources, people will always attempt to gain an edge by pushing or exceeding established limits.

But there is a fine line between outright cheating and gaining an edge. And that line is not always clear; there is an ethical component involved in a world that isn't black and white. But for the purposes of this chapter, I am advocating remaining on the side that stretches the boundaries rather than obliterates them. Once again, this maxim should not be taken literally.

That's why it's a bad saying. I am by no means advocating actual cheating. I believe that if you do take this saying at face value, it's not only unethical, but dangerous. I teach my children good sportsmanship and advocate for ethical behavior across all domains. True cheating is not a good thing and should not be rewarded as such. In fact, it should continue to be stigmatized as unacceptable behavior.

With those caveats in mind, we'll discuss this maxim from a figurative standpoint. I embrace the idea of pushing limits and boundaries and view it more as a call to creativity than breaking the rules. Find the boundaries and limits, and ethically push up against them. Think more in terms of "if you aren't thinking creatively, you aren't thinking." Or the overused saying, "Think outside the box."

Understanding the "box" you operate within is the first and most crucial step. If you are unsure of the rules, how can you push them? If you don't know where the line is, how can you color outside its edges? It sounds obvious, but it's all too often overlooked. Not fully understanding your constraints can lead to assuming you are confined in a space you actually aren't. Or, on the flip side, not realizing rules and laws are even being broken. At best, each of those scenarios places you at a competitive disadvantage; at worst, they subject you to harsh punishments.

If you're an athlete or coach, it's imperative to know every minute detail of your sport and league. A businessman must understand the laws and regulations policing his industry. A lawyer needs to have a firm grasp of case law in their specialty. A real estate agent should know every street, school, and neighborhood in their area, on top of the laws, rules, and regulations governing the industry.

After you recognize and appreciate the confines of the proverbial box you are working within, it's time to question everything you know about that box. The box is the metaphorical area that encompasses the status quo. The same old thinking, the same results, and the acceptance of long-held assumptions as facts. Question those assumptions by thinking in terms of possibilities, not probabilities.

In order to think creatively and in possibilities, you need to get rid of preconceived notions. Creative thinking places primacy on the *quantity* of ideas, not the *quality*. Initially, you need to suspend judgment and toss all sorts of ideas out there. Explore the range of options, and open the thinking space to all possibilities. After you've recognized many innovative and differing ideas as even remote possibilities, you can move on to the critical-thinking phase.

Now look at each idea with an open mind. Begin to judge the efficacy of it. Discard ideas that are too far outside the limits and rules you are working with. Combine ideas. Tweak them. Even if you don't settle on any of them as new, groundbreaking methodology in your domain, the exercise alone will get you thinking outside your box. Often, coming back from the extremes will make slight stretches more implementable.

Think about the examples we've talked about in earlier chapters of businesses that couldn't see outside of the box. Block-buster, Polaroid, and Kodak had a hard time imagining the possibilities or at least committing to pursuing them. I'd argue there are industries and jobs in front of us right now that are on the cusp of either adapting or dying.

Realtors come to mind immediately. Some real estate agents are beginning to adapt, but are they doing it soon enough? With the advent of Zillow, Redfin, and countless other online tools, buyers and sellers are more informed and doing more of the work. The 6 percent commission box is ripe for disruption. Soon enough an Amazon-like entity (or maybe even Amazon) is going to come along and go for volume and reduce total commissions to 2 or 3 percent or just charge flat fees. It's already beginning to happen. How long before the traditional real estate agent is gone?

What other industries, organizations, or products do you think are stuck in boxes of their own making? The combustion engine and shopping malls are easy targets and likely going the way of the dodo bird. Go a little further outside of box. What about smartphones? Hard to imagine them going away, but they will. *Nothing* lasts forever.

Even the "box" that we are focusing so hard on thinking outside of needs an imaginative set of eyes. The box isn't really a box. It's amorphous, with different entrances and exits and holes. Only when you fully understand the rules and confines you are operating within can you look for, identify, and exploit those loopholes.

There are times when we feel limited by assumed rules. These limitations can be artificially placed upon us by ourselves or outside influences. Someone tells us their interpretation of the rules, and we take it as fact. Often it just isn't true. It's important to challenge those preconceived notions and not just do things the way they have always been done simply *because* that's the way they've always been done.

Let's use the marijuana example again. Society has placed it in a box for decades. As discussed, we've always been told that marijuana is 100 percent bad and there is no redeeming use for it. Lately, that convention has been challenged. Promarijuana advocacy has moved light-years forward in a relatively short period of time. It's done so in a series of smaller steps, proving that stretching rules is much more effective than obliterating them.

The lobbying effort kicked off at a grassroots (pardon the pun) level. They started by espousing the health benefits of cannabis and advocating its use for medicinal purposes. After success in that arena, they began lobbying sympathetic politicians in more liberal areas to decriminalize marijuana possession and use. These efforts have now reached a point where marijuana is now completely legal in twelve states and the District of Columbia. (Federal law remains unchanged, and of course there are restrictions like age and weight.) The other states have a mix of laws ranging from decriminalizing marijuana, allowing medicinal marijuana, and keeping it illegal, but only in eight states is possessing marijuana completely illegal right now. The lines have clearly moved. Knowing where the lines are is essential in innovating past them.

In the SEAL Teams, we did everything we could to create an unfair advantage against the enemy. War is life and death, and we looked for every creative way to defeat our enemy within the laws of war.

Unlike our primary enemies of the past two decades, we were beholden to the laws and rules of war. And those rules and laws were always changing, often drastically. From how, when, where, and what kind of bomb we could drop on a target to who had to give permission for it to be dropped, the rules differed with each administration, each location, and even with each deployment. How we went after targets changed from blowing in a wall in the middle of the night to knocking on the front door in broad daylight. Even the type of ammunition we could use and who could use it was prescribed in rules and regulations. Frangible ammunition (think hollow-point-type stuff) was deemed inhumane, then it wasn't, then it was again. Then it was allowed only by exception for specific types of missions. You can't use booby traps or stay behind munitions, but you can drop a two-thousand-pound bomb on someone's head. The list goes on and on.

It was imperative that our command, our leadership, down to each enlisted operator going out on missions, fully understood those rules and abided by them. It could be the difference between being arrested and thrown in the brig for war crimes or getting a medal pinned on your chest for heroism. Dealing with the constantly shifting box was frustrating beyond belief. It defied common sense and often seemed arbitrary and capricious. While we lived within these confines, we worked as hard as we could to push up against them. We would spend a couple of heartbeats bitching about the stupidity or craziness of whatever new rule or regulation was creating the box, then get to work looking for ways to get out of it, redraw its boundaries, or erase the box entirely. We spent hours working to appreciate whatever particular box we were dealing with at the time. I sat for hours with lawyers, bosses, and teammates trying to figure out the boundaries. What were assumptions, and what were facts?

Where did the boundaries come from? What was the history behind the box? Was it new or old? Did it even exist as I imagined it? Ask yourself these questions and you may be surprised not only at what you discover but what changes you'll be able to make to further your advantage.

Without going into too many details, suffice it to say that many of the units I was a part of had special rules, different equipment, exemptions to policies, different rules of engagement, or simply appeared to be operating in a different box than everyone else. The truth is that we *were* operating in a different box than everyone else. This was often a point of contention or friction with other units or commanders on the battlefield. What they didn't get was that we didn't get those exemptions or exceptions just because we were labeled "special." Admittedly, that did play a part, but mostly we got them because we worked for them. We did the grunt work, advocated for ourselves, and got creative to change the box. We didn't accept the status quo, and we fought to change it.

Remember, if you're not thinking creatively, you're not thinking. One time we had been assigned a training mission during our reconnaissance and surveillance block of training. It entailed watching and reporting on an "enemy" force positioned on the beach. This particular "enemy" was a US Army unit practicing beach operations. They had set up an operating base that was partially on the beach butting up against the forest. Our job for the next three days would be to get as much information on their activities as possible, including pictures and video.

The enemy consisted of around seventy-five personnel. Their location made it extremely difficult to get close. One of our training cadre also let us know that he had told the enemy unit we would be out there watching and had offered a case of beer to any of them who caught us.

Great, we loved a challenge. Deep in the woods, about a kilometer away, we set up an ORP (objective rally point), which is basically an area far enough away from the objective that we could safely move about, set up communications, and rest without too much worry that the enemy would stumble on us. From there we sent out four-man reconnaissance teams to find places to set up and observe the objective. We moved only at night, very slowly and as quietly as possible. After a while, the recon teams began to report back that enemy patrols were wandering all along the edges of the forest and up and down the beach. My guys could get pretty close at night but were confident that if they stayed in the same positions during the day, they would be compromised.

We positioned one element to the north and one to the south, far enough down the beach on the edge of the woods that they could get decent images with a long-focal-length camera, but the angle was limited. It was something, but not good enough. Time to get creative.

We knew this was training, and while we didn't want to fail, if there was a time to push the boundaries, it was when the "enemy" was shooting blanks and not bullets. We discussed sneaking across the beach and getting into the water to take pictures from there as well. OK, we were more than capable of doing that, so we did. But it would still only give us night imagery. It would only be half the picture. We needed to know what was going on during the day as well. Then one of our guys broke out a map.

"Look at this," he said. "There's a convenience store about two miles south of here. Why don't two of us go down there, buy some beach shorts, touristy t-shirts, and flip-flops, and just walk right up the beach?"

Talk about getting outside the box. Why hadn't we thought of that earlier? We always carried credit cards and some cash just in case, so off they went. A few hours later, my elements watching from the south came over the radio laughing their asses off. They could see the two guys strolling right down the middle of beach with a couple of girls they had met, all drinking out of red Solo cups, laughing and talking. They strolled right up to the "enemy" unit and got the girls to pose with a bunch of them. They even took a picture of the enemy commander with the girls. They stayed for a good hour, taking pictures the whole time. Time to rinse and repeat. We did the same thing for the next two days while rotating guys around.

During the exercise debrief, the "enemy" commander was confident that we never got anywhere close to his position. We showed him the pictures and information we had gathered at night. He was pretty impressed and couldn't believe we'd gotten as close as we had. Next we showed him the pictures we took from the water each night. He was dumbstruck and even more impressed. Then we showed him the day reconnaissance results. At first he couldn't figure out how we did it. Once we told him what we had done, he was no longer impressed. He was furious, cursing at us and calling us a bunch of cheaters, then stormed out.

The regular army guys who lost that exercise considered what we had done cheating. We disagreed. We saw our approach as a creative way to solve a problem while skirting—not breaking—the rules en route to mission success. It was a gray area. I've noticed when debates arise about whether something is cheating or not, whoever lost generally defines the actions as cheating, while the winner calls them thinking outside the box. Often there is no absolute answer. It's nebulous, simply a matter of opinion. So how can you determine if a suggested solution is creative and outside-the-box thinking or goes past that standard?

A good exercise is to play out the scenario in your head beforehand. Go through your proposed actions and the opponent's reactions. If your approach is crossing the line, more often than not, you will eventually be found out, and there will be consequences. If your tactics are discovered, what will the repercussions be? Will you have to forfeit something? The game, a contract, or relationship? A good rule of thumb: If there is a punishment and you lose your gains, that is cheating. If you retain your gains and there is a perception of creativity, then you're on the right side of the debate.

There was a period in the cycling world when it was pretty much accepted that everyone doped. Even Lance Armstrong, by far the most popular and revered cyclist in the world, eventually admitted he had cheated after staunchly claiming innocence his entire career. In cycling, the box had moved. In order to compete, athletes thought they had no choice but to take performance-enhancing drugs. But did the ends justify the means? If they had played the "what if" scenario from above, would they still have done it? Again, if you do cheat, more often than not, it will eventually be discovered. Did cyclists properly analyze those repercussions? Armstrong, for one, was completely disgraced when he was finally caught. He received a lifetime ban from all sports that follow the World Anti-Doping Code and had his seven Tour de France titles stripped. Only he can say if it was worth it.

Clearly there is a fine line between creativity and cheating. As long as you know where the line is, I would argue that it should be everyone's goal to push the line as much as possible. But it can be easy to go too far.

Look at the college admissions scandal. Rich, famous parents used their considerable resources to bribe college officials and inflate test scores to secure admission to prestigious universities for their children. Instead, they could have used those resources on tutors, instructors, and coaches to help their children earn better grades, test scores, and extracurriculars. But it was easier to Photoshop images of their children rowing and to fake scores. When they got caught, what they lost far exceeded what had been gained from cheating.

There's an aspect of flexibility in ever-changing environments. Like the evolution of the marijuana advocacy, circumstances change. What was once against the law, outside the norm, or breaking the rules may no longer be considered cheating. Just as it is important to understand the constraints, it's equally important to know when they no longer apply. It's about improving your situation with the times.

There was a particularly brutal exercise that was a favorite of the instructors at BUD/S called the eight-count body builder. It's the hellish cousin and likely predecessor of the infamous burpee so familiar to fitness fanatics these days. The eight-count body builder is done just as the name implies, in eight steps. You begin in the standing position, arms at your sides, feet shoulder width apart. On count one, drop into a squat, placing your hands on the ground in front of you. Count two, kick your feet back so you're in the up position of a push-up. Count three, execute the downward portion of a push-up. Count four, execute the upward portion of the push-up back to a plank position. Count five, kick both legs out to the sides like doing a jumping jack while in the push-up position. Count six, bring your legs back together to return to the plank. Count seven, draw your legs back up to the squat position with hands in front of you (same position at count two). Count eight, leap out of the squat position, arms straight above your head and feet leaving the ground. That's one repetition of the infamous eight-count bodybuilder. This works your arms, back, chest, shoulders, and legs. It uses plyometric stretching and contraction, requires strength and stamina, improves agility, and above all builds mental toughness. This exercise was dreaded by all. It wasn't uncommon to be punished with sets of twenty-five, fifty, or even a hundred, sometimes on the hard concrete of the grinder, sometimes in the soft sand of Silver Strand.

After one of our dives in second phase, we were prepping our dive rigs for the next dive, filling out dive logs, and looking forward to the end of the day. It was about five in the afternoon, and we were in a pretty good mood because another day was nearly behind us. That would all change in a moment. One of the instructors poked his head out of the second-phase cadre office and wasn't happy with us for whatever reason. We didn't fill out the dive logs right, or our performance on the dive was crappy, or we were having too much fun. Didn't really matter. They could always find something to hammer you for. ("Hammered" was our name for the intense physical punishments we were constantly being subjected to.) It was all part of the game. No malice on the part of the instructors; it was all done by design to weed out the weak of body and mind.

Anyway, this particular instructor ranted and raved at us for a bit and then said before we could go home, we owed him one thousand eight-counts. A thousand!? We just stood there dumbfounded. After a moment, we spread out into ranks, with the class leader in front, and began the brutal task. The instructor watched us for the first twenty or so, then got bored and told us, "Keep going, gents, I'll be back." He then walked back inside through the classroom and into his office.

In general, you can knock out about ten eight-counts in a minute and a half or so. That quickly slows to two or three minutes as you tire and try to pace yourself. One hundred eight-counts straight through can easily take twenty minutes to a half hour to finish and is utterly exhausting and painful. Five hundred eight-counts, even with rests in between, is insane. A thousand eight-counts is right up there with Dante's last circle of hell. It could easily take three to five hours. This was our box for the immediate future, and we had resigned ourselves to just getting it done. Every twenty-five or so, we would take a one- or two-minute break. Right around the second or third break, one of the guys decided we were looking at the box all wrong. He came over to all the boat crew leaders and said he had an idea. "All right," we said, "let's hear it."

While we were talking, we put a lookout at the door to let us know if the instructor was coming back so we could get back to doing the exercise. He would pop in and out randomly to check in on us, and we knew we had better be doing eight-counts or he would tack on more to the tally.

One of our guys said, "Look, there's about thirty or so of us here, right?"

"Go on," we said.

"Well, Instructor Jackwagon didn't say we *each* had to do a thousand eight-counts. He said *we* had to do a thousand eight-counts. The way I figure it, we've already done about fifteen hundred eight-counts."

Now this was thinking outside the box. We liked it, but weren't sure the instructor would go for our logic. So we came up with a plan. We would keep watch on the door, catch up on prepping our dive rigs, do some stretching, and just generally relax for the next hour or so. Whenever the lookout by the door saw the instructor coming, we would quickly line back up and begin again, starting the count a couple of hundred repetitions higher than the last time we saw the instructor.

At this point, even though there was a risk of even more hammering if we were caught, everyone was on board. We were technically complying with the instructor's orders; we had just expanded our thinking space. We got creative. After a couple of hours, the instructor came back out, and we counted out the final reps and reported complete. He looked at us sideways, took a couple of steps between the ranks, eyeing several guys up and down, walked back up in front of the class, and in a normal voice said, "Good job, dismissed." We breathed a collective sigh of relief and got the hell out of there as fast as we could.

I never found out if the instructor knew exactly what we did, but he had to know that we hadn't each done a thousand eight-counts. Was it an intentional lesson in getting outside the box, thinking creatively, and working as team? Or was it by chance? Doesn't really matter. The lesson remains. You need to look at each challenge ahead of you from multiple angles and perspectives. There are often solution sets that aren't initially obvious, but by looking at problems with an unconstrained, open, and creative mind-set and exploring possibilities, you'll be surprised at the innovative approaches that appear.

Every day I'm amazed and refreshed by the amount of creativity that I see as we progress through this global pandemic and the new reality of physical distancing. The people and businesses that accept that the box has changed, embrace it instead of lament it, and get creative are the ones who will come out of this pandemic stronger and thriving.

Then there are others I see who view the situation as if it is a movie on pause, and when someone hits play, the movie will pick up where it had stopped. It won't. That isn't a good or bad thing, it just is. If you are going to push the bounds and get creative, you first have to recognize the box that you're in and set out to not only discover the limits but also to escape the box. Remember, if you're not thinking creatively, you're not thinking.

17

THE ONLY EASY DAY
WAS YESTERDAY

It was the third and final phase of BUD/S training. We could see
the light at the end of the tunnel. But it was far from over. Once
again we found ourselves subjected to a pretty grueling hammer
session. I think this particular session was set off because we
forgot to include one of the instructors' surfboards when we
loaded the plane to head over to San Clemente Island. To say that
he was pissed off was an understatement. The other instructors
actually felt bad for us. We all linked arms and proceeded into
the frosty Pacific. The offended instructor would bring us to
the edge of hypothermia, back onto the beach for eight-counts,
then back into the water. Over and over again. This lasted for
hours. But at this point of training, we no longer cared. Nobody
was quitting. You could kill us, but you couldn't hurt us.

By the time the instructor pulled us out of the water for the last time, we were at the edges of consciousness, exhausted beyond belief, and shaking uncontrollably. I remember him speaking to us in a more fatherly voice. "Gents, this is nothing. If, and I stress *if*, you make it to the SEAL Teams, you will be colder, hotter, more exhausted, and more challenged than you ever were here at BUD/S. Remember, the only easy day was yesterday."

At the time, I didn't believe a word he said and wrote it off to bluster and hyperbole. Shortly after, I would find myself at graduation, beginning my journey in the SEAL Teams. During that journey, that instructor's words would prove true time and time again. Whether it was swimming in forty-degree water in the Beagle Channel off the coast of Tierra Del Fuego and the southernmost city in the world, Ushuaia, Argentina, while conducting a hydrographic reconnaissance, baking in the scorching 120-degree heat of Middle East deserts, patrolling up the insanely steep hills of Kosovo or Afghanistan, or not sleeping for days on a regular basis, I can assure you that I was definitely colder, hotter, more exhausted, and more challenged than I ever was in BUD/S. The only easy day truly was yesterday.

What an appropriate bookend (pun intended).

If you've done the work and adopted the mind-set outlined in the first sixteen maxims, this last one should come as little surprise. By now you know I'm not offering easy solutions to life's problems. There is no silver bullet within these pages, no answers to the test. Only guidance toward hard work and critical and creative thinking. This final saying encapsulates that.

As with most of the sayings we have been exploring, "The only easy day was yesterday" is not meant to be taken literally. It isn't concrete. It's an intangible idea communicated in a gray world, conveying several different thoughts and ideas. In the simplest terms, it means that yesterday was easy only because it's over.

But when taken at face value, it can be interpreted as meaning life only gets harder with each subsequent sunrise. That's a simplistic interpretation that carries a negative connotation. That's not how I see it. I look at this saying as a positive, articulating the opportunity to continue moving forward and growing. Difficulty is relative—what was once hard is now easy. Once a task is finished, it's time to find the next challenge and up the difficulty. The only easy day was yesterday.

This is how growth is achieved. Without challenge there is no progress. Once you've overcome or learned something, it's time to introduce more difficult and uncomfortable tasks. And on it goes. There is no end state apart from constant growth. Continued challenges—and even pain—are requirements for continued improvement. That's what all our maxims are about: Challenging yourself in order to grow. Getting comfortable being uncomfortable.

Sometimes bad things are going to happen. The death of a loved one, losing a job, getting sick, a global pandemic that shuts down the economy: these are all real and almost inevitable parts of being a human. The only easy day was yesterday isn't meant to suggest that what comes next will be worse or harder than those things. It means that because they're over—because you got past them, you survived, you became stronger because of them—they're now easy. Only what remains to tackle is hard.

This maxim is about moving forward with a future-oriented viewpoint. About learning from the past rather than dwelling on it. About stating the obvious: yesterday is over. The past is the past. There is nothing you can do about it; you have to move on to the next day. You can't drive a car by looking in the rearview mirror. The past may be necessary for appreciating your environment, but you must spend the bulk of your time watching the road ahead.

However, you do need to occasionally glance in the rearview mirror for reference. This contributes to situational awareness and gives you an appreciation for the context and environment you're operating in. You cannot change yesterday, but you can take lessons from it and apply them to today.

Naturally there is a caveat to this. Often we get bogged down and make assumptions that because the road in the rearview is straight, the road ahead will be as well. While innately we know that isn't true, cognitive biases can trick us into operating as if the future will be the same as the past. It won't be.

Just as you can't change the past, you can't know what the future will bring. That arrow-straight road in the rearview could easily change to wet and slick curves ahead. What's behind you is done—hence, easy. The focus must be on navigating those curves in front of you.

Over the years since I retired, I've had the opportunity to work with people, either through nonprofits or individually, that are transitioning from the military to the civilian sector. This is a difficult process and a serious challenge. The men and women taking off their uniforms are starting down a new road that looks nothing like the one in the rearview mirror. Many of them cling to the past like a security blanket. Oftentimes they find themselves right back in a similar job to the one they did in the military, working as a contractor, the only difference is a suit and tie instead of a uniform. If that path is truly what they want, more power to them. But I know that many want something different yet have a hard time lifting the anchor keeping them stuck in place. They have an incredible amount to offer the civilian sector but have difficulty translating and verbalizing what they did in the military to the language of the civilian sector. And the civilian sector isn't well educated enough about the military and the various units, jobs, and skills inherent. The civilian sector often looks at the military as a monolithic entity when it's anything but. The sailor, soldier, or airman making the leap often doesn't know what they want to do, or they might not understand the options open to them. This is the new road ahead, filled with twists and turns but endless opportunity as well. It simply takes raising the anchor and getting the ship moving.

You can look at the complexity of the world like a sailor at sea. The sailor can't control the ocean. He can't control the tides or waves or storms. He can only navigate each external factor the best he can.

He can ensure he is operating a seaworthy vessel. He can prepare by reading the tide charts and monitoring the weather. Prepping the boat to have everything he needs. Putting contingency and emergency plans in place. Making sure his lines are stowed. All the things to give him the best shot at safely reaching his destination.

But the sailor can't be lured into a false sense of security. No matter what preparations are made, the sea—and world—is an ambiguous and unpredictable environment. He can't eliminate all risk. The days ahead are going to be challenging. They're going to be hard.

That doesn't have to be a bad thing. "Hard" is not synonymous with "miserable." Hard can be fun. Hard can be rewarding, and often it is. When you learn to embrace and love challenges, "hard" isn't a traumatic or miserable experience, it's a fulfilling one.

Probably the most fulfilling—while also challenging—thing I've done is have kids. If you have kids, you know what I'm talking about. When you first brought home your little helpless human, if you are anything like me, you probably didn't have any idea what the hell you were doing. The highs and lows and twists and turns come at a breakneck pace. One moment your little girl or boy looks angelic, sleeping peacefully, and the next they are screaming in a tone and pitch that physically hurts and seems like it will never end. And so it goes for years, the highest highs and some of the lowest lows. Through it all, you are growing just as much as they are.

One of my favorite speeches by one of my favorite guys (mostly because he cracks me up) was a commencement address delivered by legendary college football coach Lou Holtz. The speech was remarkable guidance for personal responsibility while emphasizing many of the same themes in this book. The gist—and most powerful line to me—is "You're either growing or you're dying." I have always believed strongly in that sentiment. Without risk, without pushing yourself, you accomplish nothing. Simply retaining the status quo is not good enough. Not growing is equivalent to dying.

I do think it's important to define growth, at least within the context we are discussing. What it boils down to is this: Are you adding value to your life or the lives of others? If not, you're dying. You're stagnant if you aren't learning anything new or adding value.

Complacency kills. Complacency kills because it kills learning and growth. You have to take risks. You have to put yourself out there. The fighter jet remains safe in the hangar, but that's not what it was made to do. It's meant to defy gravity at breakneck speeds, push the limits of technology and human capability, and engage an adversary in a deadly dance in the air.

It was a huge risk going to BUD/S and trying to get to the SEAL Teams. If I hadn't made it through training, I would have been stuck on a ship my whole career, with no real say as to what I did in the navy. It would have been a devastating blow that would have changed the trajectory of my life and career.

But taking that enormous risk provided untold rewards. For me it was worth it. Becoming a special operator, a member of what I considered an elite unit, was my passion. I fully dedicated myself to that pursuit, and as far as I was concerned, there was no chance I wouldn't make it.

But as we know, there is no end state. There is no "making it." Once I got to the SEAL Teams, I couldn't remain complacent. There's another saying in the Teams: "Earn your Trident every day." This is a corollary of "the only easy day was yesterday." It's not what you did yesterday that matters; it's what you do today that counts. There is no resting on your laurels. You have to prove your value every day.

It was time for the next challenge. That progression was to screen for DEVGRU (Naval Special Warfare Development Group), ███████████████████████████████████████ ████████████. It was the next level and challenge in front of me.

I didn't *have* to go that route. The majority of guys in the SEAL Teams have successful and fulfilling careers without ever going to that command. Nobody forces it on you; like going to the SEAL Teams, you have to *really* want it. And if I wanted to go to DEVGRU, I'd have to undergo another rigorous selection process. Think another BUD/S for those who are already SEALs, but different. ██

███████████████████████████. Then, if I did make it through, I would be a new guy all over again. Virtually nothing I had accomplished previously in the SEAL Teams would carry over to my new command. I had been a SEAL for around nine years at the time. I like to think I had a good reputation. I'd done a bunch of deployments, had honed my operational and leadership skills, and was at the top of my game. But at DEVGRU I'd have the least experience of anyone there and would start at the bottom of the totem pole. I would have to learn a whole new set of skills and prove myself all over again. Still, this seemed like the obvious and only path for me. It was the next summit to climb. Why? Because of the challenge. Because it was an opportunity to grow. Right or wrong, this unit was considered the Everest of the SEAL Teams. Not only did I want the challenge, but I wanted to be around people and other SEALs who also wanted that challenge. It was a different culture and unique brotherhood. This isn't a value judgment or implication that anyone at DEVGRU is better than anyone at other SEAL Teams. They're just different.

When I did get there, I knew I had to be humble. I had to put my ego in check and say, "OK, I am going to have to start new and learn again." There were challenges every day. I'd overcome one, put it in the rearview, and move on to the next. I understood that what I did yesterday only mattered in context and didn't prove where I would go tomorrow. I truly had to earn my Trident every day.

It's the same in life or business. Once you get the job you're interviewing for, you can't become content. You need to tackle the next challenge, whatever it may be. Start with learning everything about your new role and company. Take higher education courses to become an expert in your field. Start working toward a promotion. Always strive for that next accomplishment.

After DEVGRU, there were plenty of new challenges and opportunities to grow ahead. My primary weapon was transitioning from a rifle to a keyboard. The end of my career in the SEAL Teams found me sitting across the desk from the secretary of defense and regularly attending one-on-one meetings with four-star generals and admirals, including the chairman of the Joint Chiefs of Staff. I transitioned from the challenge of the relatively straightforward battlefields of Afghanistan and Iraq to the complexities of navigating the halls of power in and around Washington, DC, where it wasn't uncommon for someone to shake your hand and at the same time stab you in the back. It was a new challenge, another summit, another opportunity to grow and learn. I was working on some unique special activities that afforded me the opportunity to sit down and have conversations with the head of the CIA, the head of NSA, the director of National Intelligence, and the National Security Council at the White House, among others pulling the strings of power in the world of national security. Eventually I retired from the navy and went into the business world. New hardships and chances for learning awaited me. Then I started my own company. I wrote this book. All were hurdles that I embraced as opportunities for growth. Because if you aren't growing, you're dying.

The trials of life should not be looked at as bad things that produce misery and pain. Just because something isn't easy doesn't mean it has to be painful. Improving yourself should be enjoyable and can become addictive.

My father started his career as a salesman for Motorola. He got promoted to area manager, then regional manager, then vice president of a division. He worked his way up to become a corporate elected officer, all because he didn't sit back and enjoy his victories. Instead of looking in the rearview, he always looked forward. To this day I remember some great advice he gave me. He said, "No promotion or new job is worth taking if you are 100 percent comfortable with it."

Growth doesn't always have to look like an upward trajectory. It isn't always a straight line from bottom to top. It's relative and subjective. Remember, the definition is adding value to your life or others'. Maybe there's a high-powered corporate executive who no longer feels fulfilled running a huge company. They've achieved what they set out to do and might even feel stagnant. So it's time to look for their next challenge. Maybe that challenge is as a high school math teacher. That's growth. It doesn't have to be measured in money or accolades.

I explained how I didn't believe my instructors in BUD/S when they said I would be colder and more exhausted if I made it to the Teams. And I told you how they were right. I'd bet that if you asked a small-business owner about their evolution, they might share a similar story.

When you first start a business, it's long hours and hard days. You wear many hats. Usually you're the first marketing manager, the CFO, the head of business development, and customer service all rolled into one. Those long hours are worked with the goal of building a successful business. The company expands to ten employees, fifty, five hundred. The owner is, in theory, able to adapt their pace and schedule to suit other priorities. They hire marketing people and accountants. However, despite delegating more and working less, most reflect on those early days as easier. Simpler. The business was less complicated then. As their skills and understanding of the business grow, so does the complexity. Issues are larger now, decisions more impactful. The only easy day was yesterday.

Looking back at it now, BUD/S actually was pretty easy. Maybe not easy. Simple. I was given my schedule each day and knew exactly what I had to do. Once I got to the Teams, it wasn't as simple. Each job was more complex and harder than the next. Responsibilities grew exponentially, but so did the feeling of accomplishment and fulfillment.

If you're standing at the base of a mountain, it probably looks like the highest mountain in the world. But the reality is, once you reach the summit, you will realize there is a whole range of higher, harder, and more fulfilling summits in front of you. The longer that I was in the SEAL Teams, the more I realized how little I knew and how much learning and potential for growth were ahead of me. That experience has not waned. This isn't any different from the civilian world or any other industry. I undergo constant challenges and find new mountains to climb every day.

Every fork you take in the path up the mountain will lead to new choices, new twists and turns, new obstacles, new lessons, new learning, and new accomplishments. Life is the ultimate adventure. The choice is yours. Do you lie down on the trail, make camp, build a cabin, and be content? Or do you press on and continue to learn and grow? You'll never know what is waiting for you around the corner. There are no guarantees. The only certainty is that the only easy day was yesterday. But by thinking smarter, not harder, you can move out of your comfort zone, develop creative approaches to challenges ahead, and build a tomorrow that's bigger and better than you've ever imagined before.

ACKNOWLEDGMENTS

I would like to offer my sincere gratitude to the following people and organizations:

To Andy, without whom this book wouldn't have been written. His writing, friendship, guidance through the process, and patience with my ramblings were invaluable.

To my publisher and all the people that made this book happen, from editing to layout and cover design, especially Nina and Naren.

To the men of Foxtrot Platoon, SEAL Team FOUR whose influence and lessons stayed with me throughout the years. I am forever grateful for the experience.

To all the frogmen, warriors, sailors, soldiers, and airmen from my various assignments who taught, mentored, counseled, led, followed, and influenced me. Special thanks to the brotherhood at TWO, FOUR, and DEVGRU.

To all of our fallen brothers and, just as importantly, to the families they've left behind. The debt of gratitude that we owe you all is immeasurable and eternal.

To my friend first, business partner second, Charlie—thank you for everything over the years. Looking forward to many more.

To Eric, Derrick, Mike, Shawn, and TJ, who keep me grounded, listen to me rant, and always bring a smile to my face and make me laugh.

To my sister whom I love and adore.

To my brother who has become my best friend, sounding board and counsel over the years. Thanks and love you.

To my mother and father, without whom none of my adventures or accomplishments would be possible. Words seem to fall short to express my gratitude for your unconditional love, support, and encouragement, so I'll keep it simple—thank you. I love you.

To my children who keep me young and are a constant source of happiness and inspiration. You impress, amaze, and fill me with joy and hope every day. I love you to the moon and back and more!

And last, but surely not least, thank you to my wife, whose love and joy knows no bounds, who stands by me no matter what, and whose very existence makes the world a better place. I love you, forever and for always.